OLDER PERSONS AND RETIREMENT COMMUNITIES

OLDER PERSONS AND
RETIREMENT COMMUNITIES

Case Studies in
Social Gerontology

By

JERRY JACOBS, Ph.D.

Department of Sociology
Syracuse University
Syracuse, New York

CHARLES C THOMAS • PUBLISHER
Springfield • *Illinois* • *U.S.A.*

Published and Distributed Throughout the World by

CHARLES C THOMAS • PUBLISHER

Bannerstone House

301-327 East Lawrence Avenue, Springfield, Illinois, U.S.A.

© *1975, by* CHARLES C THOMAS • Publisher

ISBN 0-398-03445-1 (cloth)

ISBN 0-398-03446-X (paper)

Library of Congress Catalog Card Number: 75-8793

Printed in the United States of America

R-1

Library of Congress Cataloging in Publication Data

Jacobs, Jerry.
    Older persons and retirement communities.

    Bibliography: p.
    1. Retirement, Places of — United States — Case
studies. I. Title.
HQ1063.J32 1975   301.43'5   75-8793
ISBN 0-398-03445-1
ISBN 0-398-03446-X (pbk.)

INTRODUCTION

IT is interesting to note that while there is considerable literature on retirement (a selected bibliography of well over one hundred references are given in this volume), one can count the number of ethnographic studies of older persons on the fingers of one hand. There are a number of reasons for this.

Since Durkheim, sociologists have been concerned with the secondary analysis of statistical data in the search for *social facts.* Survey research, demographic studies and the analysis of official statistics on a broad range of topics have been the traditional concerns of sociology, not only within the area of gerontology, but with respect to other social phenomena as well.

While sociologists have generally avoided field studies, the works of anthropologists have been steeped in this tradition. However, the ethnographies of anthropologists have almost always been concerned with other cultures.

Psychologists, too, while they study individuals in their own culture, have been concerned with questions other than those dealt with in ethnographic studies. For example, these works frequently concern themselves with personality changes in later life, psychological adjustment to retirement, cognitive ability or unconscious motivations.

Finally, those in the helping professions have oriented their efforts more toward such problems as how to improve the psychological and physical well-being of the elderly rather than research questions dealing with the current status of older persons.

As a result, the social sciences currently have very little in the way of descriptive accounts of the everyday life of older retired persons in their natural settings based upon unobtrusive observations of those activities over time. Not only is there a lack of material dealing with what older persons do, but there is even less to indicate what these activities meant to the participants at the time and in the settings in which they occurred. Indeed, the three ethnographies in this volume represent the bulk of the literature in the field as it relates to the question of what older persons do and what these activities mean to them in the context of contemporary American society.

It is perhaps not surprising to find that accompanying this paucity of field studies on older persons is the almost complete lack of theory in gerontological literature. If social theory is seen to result (within a scientific framework) from observation, description, catagorization and synthesis of social actions and the meaning of social actions, then the absence of theories of aging is in no way enigmatic. As things now stand, the descriptive data needed to take the first step in such a theory-building process is almost completely absent.

What follows in the remainder of this volume is intended to rectify the problem by providing some initial insight into the question of retirement and retirement settings and a basis for a *grounded theory* of aging.

Those interested in the literature on retirement from other than an ethnographic perspective are referred to the bibliography at the end of the book, and particularly to those review articles set off by asterisks.

Before entering into a discussion and analysis of the data, the author opens with a methodological note on High Heaven and the other case studies found in Chapters II and III. All were conducted from a participant observational orientation which incorporates the general theoretical perspective of *symbolic interaction*. In sociology this methodological orientation has traditionally taken the form of *field studies,* while in cultural anthropology it has taken the form of ethnography.

Allowing that ethnographies usually describe and analyze other cultures, a more recent and growing body of anthropological research has been concerned with the contemporary

American scene.* The sociological orientation to field studies has its roots in the early works of George Hebert Mead, John Horton Cooley and Herbert Blumer, and in the later works of Anselm Strauss and Erving Goffman to mention but a few.

Basically it takes the position that in order to understand social phenomena, the researcher needs to discover the actor's *definition of the situation,* i.e. his perception and interpretation of reality and how this relates to his behavior. Further, the actor's perception of reality turns upon his ongoing interpretation of the social interactions of which he partakes, which in turn pivots upon his use of symbols in general, and language in particular. Finally, in order for the researcher to come to such an understanding he must be able (albeit imperfectly) to put himself in the other man's shoes through empathy. From this perspective, social meanings (which direct human behavior) do not adhere in the interactions, institutions or social objects themselves. Rather, meanings are conferred upon social events by the actor who must first interpret what is going on from the social context in which these events occur. This emerging gestalt (the "definition of the situation")† is seen to result from the interplay of biography, situation and linguistic exchange that characterizes all social exchanges, nonverbal communications not withstanding.

In order to understand this process and the forms of social interaction that result from it, the researcher invoking the participant observational orientation often, but not always seeks to interact with the actors, observe and partake of their activities, conduct informal interviews with them and others who are or were party to the social environment under study, and tries, through the above involvements and general orientation, to reconstruct the reality of the individuals involved. If successful,

---

*For example, a current series in cultural anthropology by Holt, Rinehart and Winston includes the following: Jacobs, *Fun City: An Ethnographic Study of a Retirement Community;* Keiser, *The Vice Lords: Warriors of the Streets;* Pilcher, *The Portland Longshoremen: A Dispersed Urban Community;* Friedland and Nelkin, *Migrant: Agricultural Workers in America's Northeast.*

†This notion was first envoked by W. I. Thomas, *The Child in America.* New York, Knopf, 1928, p. 584.

the researcher acquires "members knowledge"* and consequently understands, from the participant's point of view, what motivated them to do what the researcher observed them doing and what these acts meant to the participants at the time they were enacted.

All of the above hopefully leads to a kind and level of insight that Max Weber referred to as "Versten,"† a plateau in sociological investigation he felt one needed to reach if he were to achieve true sociological understanding. It is within this methodological orientation and these theoretical guidelines that the current studies were undertaken.

The study of High Heaven was officially begun in September of 1972. However, access to the site, a precondition for beginning the observations, participation and interviews, was not actually achieved until December, 1972. It took about four months of negotiations and numerous meetings with the housing authority, The Tenants Research Committee of High Heaven, the university and other interested parties to gain official and *de facto* access to the setting. The author's direct involvement with the students and the residents of High Heaven and the resulting data were gathered between December, 1972, and February, 1974. The analysis and interpretation of the data, an ongoing process, was continued from February, 1974, until the present.

The data are comprised of hundreds of hours of observations of varying durations conducted on different days and times of day throughout the academic year at High Heaven, the students' dining hall and the student dorms. The descriptions of residents' activities and the nature of their social involvements with other residents and/or students and what these interactions or the lack of them meant to the residents and students were recorded in writing or recorded on tape and then transcribed as soon as possible after they were observed. In addition to these written records based upon direct observation and informal discussions, there was a set of tape recorded interviews with thirty-five

---

*For a discussion of members' knowledge see Harold Garfinkle, Studies in Ethnomethodology, Englewood Cliffs, Prentice Hall, 1967.

†For a discussion of verstehen see Max Weber, *The Theory of Social and Economic Organization*, New York, The Free Press, 1964, p. 88.

residents conducted in their apartments and scheduled with their consent and at their convenience. These taped interviews were transcribed, and they constituted another important source of data. Finally, interviews were conducted with former employees, students and others who had participated in the experiment in intergenerational living described in this work. Diaries of participating students and the accounts of outside third parties were also utilized. This same basic approach was used by the author in the study of *Fun City* and by Arlie Hochschild in the study of *Merrill Court*.

The need for this kind of descriptive and analytical studies of the everyday lives of older persons in natural settings is obvious.* Without such firsthand studies conducted over time, an accurate assessment of the needs and expectations of the older persons is impossible. (The number of retirement-age persons has increased 538 percent since the turn of the century.) The lack of accurate assessments of this kind will result in the extension of play-it-by-ear planning, the unanticipated outcomes of which are described here and in other studies by the author.† Allowing that all prediction of social phenomena is, and is likely to remain, imperfect, there is presently much room for improvement, especially within the gerontological literature. The author is hopeful that the insights derived from the current study will enhance not only our capacity for predicting outcomes in planned retirement communities, but also our understanding from the participants' point of view of why such undertakings succeed or fail.

---

*While there is extensive literature on aging and a considerable amount of literature on retirement, few of these studies are in the ethnographic tradition. Some notable exceptions of ethnographies of the aged within the contemporary American scene are Jerry Jacobs, *Fun City: An Ethnographic Study of a Retirement Community*, New York, Holt, Rinehart and Winston, 1974; Arlie Russell Hockschild, *The Unexpected Community*, Englewood Cliffs, Prentice-Hall, 1973; and James Spradley, *You Owe Yourself a Drunk*, Boston, Little, Brown, 1970.

†*Fun City: An Ethnographic Study of a Retirement Community*, New York, Holt, Rinehart and Winston, 1974.

CONTENTS

OLDER PERSONS AND
RETIREMENT COMMUNITIES

Chapter I

HIGH HEAVEN: A CASE STUDY

AIMS AND INTENTIONS

H IGH Heaven was initially conceived of as a kind of pilot demonstration project designed to find ways of integrating the activities of university students and the *well-elderly* who would reside in separate but adjacent facilities. The study was designed to find helpful methods for overcoming some of the untoward effects currently associated with aging, and, more specifically with *intergenerational differences.* It was further anticipated that a partial integration of social activities would be possible in spite of the age, educational and class differences that characterized the university students and the residents.

It was hypothesized that through shared interactions the students and older persons would get to know one another, and that a better understanding of the other's problems, life styles and ideologies would foster greater tolerance. Greater tolerance would, in turn, help break down the negative stereotyping that currently exists between youth and older persons which contributes toward the creation of intergenerational differences. Finally, this accomplished, it was expected that the students and retired persons would be able to initiate and sustain meaningful forms of interactions that would be viewed as reciprocally beneficial.

THE SITE

High Heaven is a twenty-one story, high-rise retirement setting located on a former cemetery site. It is situated in a middle-size eastern city in the downtown area, adjacent to a black ghetto. It was the first retirement complex of its kind to be located on a campus. It is federally subsidized and administered to initially by the city housing authority and the university, and caters to *depression era* low income persons of low educational achievement; they are recruited primarily from the city proper and neighboring towns, and are either natives of the area or long-term residents.

The entire complex — High Heaven, the student dorms located across the quad, the university's gerontology center, and the student-resident dining hall was planned as early as 1960 as the first campus-based student-older person living complex in the county but was not completed and occupied until late 1969. There are three kinds of apartments available to the tenants, one-room apartments, one-bedroom apartments and two-bedroom apartments. Each of the floors has the same basic plan. There are a total of 364 apartments that house approximately 420 residents. The rent the tenants pay is calculated on a sliding scale. The rental range per apartment is as follows: studio — $40.00-$80.00, streamline — $46.00-$86.00, and galaxie — $56.00-$96.00 per month.

There were some unusual features included in this first in subsidized public housing for the elderly. For example, the first three floors of the building were devoted to meeting the social and physical needs of the residents. The first floor contained a lounge, the mail boxes, a large social room and two offices. The second floor housed a large room used for planned social events, a kitchen that allowed for food preparation on special occasions such as holiday parties, a men's club room, women's club room, library and chapel. The third floor was a facility run by the county public health department that was not operational until the end of 1971, and was used for screening residents of High Heaven (to see that they were among the well elderly, provide peripheral health care to residents upon orders from the residents' (outside) physicians, and screen other potential tenants for appropriate placement outside of High Heaven in the many other facilities administered by the city housing authority.

While the students did not actually live in High Heaven and the elderly did not live in the dorms, they did share to some extent certain facilities and activities from 1969 to 1970, or during what some residents referred to as the *golden era*. The following is a description of this shared social life, how it was initiated and how it abruptly terminated.

THE ROLE OF THE UNIVERSITY: THE GOLDEN ERA

This period represented an effort on the university's part to conduct a small-scale social experiment in intergenerational living. It was funded by a grant administered by the dean of the school of social work, and provided a paid person with a master's degree in social work who was especially trained to act as the coordinator of social services for High Heaven. The social work coordinator actually lived in the building, and his office was a desk located in the middle of the social room on the first floor. He proved to be not only an able organizer, but a dedicated and untiring advocate of the residents' causes. The grant also funded a second M.S.W. who acted as *training director* for the five graduate social work students who were an integral part of the project. High Heaven served for them as a field placement and part of their training program. The *magnificent seven,* as they came to be referred to by some of the residents under the direction of the dean of the school of social work, comprised the total university work force involved directly with the residents. This small but effective group was responsible during the year and a half of its existence for establishing a variety of resident-student interactions, and, more specifically, in helping the residents to organize a number of active and meaningful in-house social organizations.

The following are some of the benefits accruing to the residents during the golden era. For example, upon first moving to High Heaven the residents moved into a building still under construction and not sufficiently funded to fulfill the designers' promise. As previously noted, the third floor was to house a kitchen, the residents' meeting room, an arts and crafts area, a men's club room, a women's club room, a library and a chapel. The main room had no drapes, carpet, chairs or tables; the kitchen had no dishes or cooking utensils, the chapel had no pews or altar; and the library was but an empty shell. By getting the students to help the residents and by organizing the residents to help themselves, the student-resident program succeeded in getting outside sources to volunteer the necessary equipment and furnishings needed to transform the third floor from a potentially useful open space into a center of social life for High Heaven.

Apart from the material benefits that accrued to the residents during this period there were the benefits that resulted from the student-resident interaction itself. These took many forms.

FORMS OF RESIDENT-STUDENT INTERACTION

One set of interactions involved the use of the student dining hall. Between twenty-five and thirty residents either routinely or occasionally shared the dining hall with students during the golden era. This was located in the university gerontology building adjacent to High Heaven. The interactions that took place there were facilitated in the following way. An arrangement was made with the university whereby residents could eat at the student dining hall at student rates which were substantially below those offered to the general public. However, this cost, while representing a good value was still more than most residents could routinely meet. Most residents continued to prepare their meals in their own apartments for much less. Interactions centering around food-related activities were therefore extended to High Heaven itself. Students and residents periodically held pot luck lunches and social get-togethers that actively involved a different segment of tenants from those who used the student dining hall. These get-togethers were usually staged on the terrace floor. On a more individual basis, residents from time to time invited one or more students to dinner in their apartments. While very few residents participated in this form of interaction even during the golden era, having had a student to dinner even on a one-time basis constituted an event that was vividly recounted years later, and for some it represented their only contact with students. Thanksgiving, Halloween and Christmas dinner parties were another series of activities that also centered directly or indirectly about food. While most students left the campus during these vacation breaks, and student participation in these parties was for this and other reasons very limited, they represented a significant happening for the residents. This aspect will be dealt with in greater detail later. These food-related activities then succeeded in promoting (if not quantitatively, then qualitatively) a good deal of meaningful interaction between students and residents.

Another activity students scheduled was a film series for the residents in the library of High Heaven. These were, by High Heaven standards, relatively well-attended, especially during that period of the series when the residents chose the films. Between thirty and fifty persons routinely packed the library on movie night. At a later stage students selected the films to be shown, and attendance dropped off markedly.

Residents and students also interacted in the snack bar. The student snack bar located on the ground floor of gerontology center, which also housed the student cafeteria, was a favorite meeting place for a number of older persons, especially during the warmer weather. This was not surprising since it provided the residents with their only air-conditioned social space. High Heaven has no air conditioning, and until last year it had no provisions for the tenant to install his own. As a result, the snack bar offered residents and students the only comfortable, convenient and neutral social space in which to spend a pleasant afternoon with friends. It was another of the fringe benefits that fell to the residents as a result of the university's involvement.

Other activities and programs that resulted from the efforts of the magnificent seven were continuing education classes taught in High Heaven; a *matching program* that matched a student volunteer with a particular resident and insured regular and prolonged contact between the two; an in-house newspaper printed on a regular basis; the organization of the High Heaven choir, and a bridge club, a chess club, a resident men's club and a women's club. While the coordinator and social work students were instrumental in initiating these programs, and their involvement with the residents was considerable in the above regard, the actual student-resident interaction at the functions themselves was minimal. Very few students participated in the residents' activities after their initial involvement in helping to organize them. By the same token, very few if any residents of High Heaven ever sought the company of the students at the dorms.

While the above might seem a modest beginning in that it actually involved relatively few students and residents, these programs need to be put into perspective. It was, after all, a start in the right direction, and one that required a prodigious effort on the part of the dean, the coordinator of social services, the director of social work training, the social work students, the students in the dorms, and the residents themselves. It was no easy matter overcoming the initial inertia that was encountered by both students and residents toward establishing and perpetuating meaningful forms of interactions. It is in this light that the program, at least during the height of its activity, can be viewed as having been relatively successful. It was certainly clear that involved residents and students tended to view the golden era in this way. All of the above transpired within approximately the first two years of High Heaven's existence.

THE END OF A PROMISING START

What is the current status of the project, and what has become of this promising start? There was a long list of events that led to the gradual disintegration of these early programs through the progressive disengagement of resident-resident, resident-student and university involvement.

To begin with, the grant supporting the coordinator of social services, the director of training and the social work students came to an end. With it ended the active participation of students and residents in the programs that had been initiated by the magnificent seven.

Another factor leading to the early demise of these programs was the fact that with the university's administrative and other disengagement from the project, the administration of High Heaven fell exclusively to the city housing authority. This, too, had many untoward consequences. The position of the housing authority was that High Heaven was only one of the many rental facilities it administered, and that it ought not to be given special treatment. The "Waldorf Astoria", as it was referred to among some housing authority personnel and the poorer white community, (the black community referred to it as "The White House"), came under attack for the special privileges and benefits that had accrued to it as a result of its placement on campus and its having initially received the university's support. With the demise of the magnificent seven the community support for the programs that the university has been instrumental in instituting did not materialize as the university had supposed it would. Rather, there was a black and white backlash from the community and from the lower income persons who comprised the population of housing authority tenants.

Another unpopular act of the housing authority was their choice in replacing the initial coordinator of social services. His replacement did not live in High Heaven, nor, in the opinion of the residents, was she as capable, dedicated or enthusiastic as the original coordinator. This, too, helped contribute to the downfall of student-resident programs. It also contributed to the residents casting the housing authority into the role of villain while the university, now much less involved administratively and otherwise with High Heaven, was, because of its prior support, viewed more positively. This resident position has persisted. The following excerpt from a tenant interview is illustrative.

Mrs. O.: I wanted to tell you something. I wish you wouldn't involve Mrs. C. (the coordinator replacement chosen by the housing authority) any more than you have to. She's not going to be any help to you.

Dr. J.: I would just as soon talk to the people in the building.

Mrs. O.: You see, she's a good, nice woman, but I think she's very neurotic. And I find that she doesn't always stand in back of what she says. I don't want to run anybody down because I think she's a good woman. She tends to be all right, but I have lost an awful lot of faith in her in a year. I tell her as little as possible now, but she twists my words around and everyone else's words around and she betrayed me. (A story of betrayal is omitted here.) She'd done it to me before, see. So I can no longer trust her.... Why do you have to go through her? Who told you you have to go through her?

Dr. J.: I don't have to. I can go to anybody that can tell me
something about life at High Heaven.

Mrs. O.: It's none of her business. What she does is run back and
tell the housing authority, "Oh, I'm so important. They
depend so on me." She makes a big thing of it. . . . There
is something; they (the housing authority) think we're
"The Hilton"; we've got too much over here. What we
have we've made ourselves, but the other buildings
administered by the housing authority are jealous of
High Heaven. But no one is going to make me forget the
dean (of the social work school), what he did for us and
Bruce T. (the original coordinator of social services).
Nobody, nobody. Mrs. C. really should have no
business; she shouldn't even stick her nose in your
business. I hope you won't go to her unless you have to
because the less she knows (the better).

Still another factor contributing to the downfall of in-house
and outside interaction for the residents of High Heaven were the
racist attitudes that one encountered among some of the upper
echelon in-house committee leaders and their influence as
opinion leaders upon the other tenants. This aspect will be dealt
with in greater detail later in the work.

Coupled with the question of racial attitudes was the problem
of security. High Heaven is located adjacent to a black ghetto.
Residents' automobiles have been vandalized, and in some
instances the residents have been mugged, robbed and/or have
sustained bodily injury at the hands of individual black youths
from the adjacent neighborhood. Allowing that there was some
real basis for residents' concern regarding security, this feature, as
it affected their life-style, took on ubiquitous proportions. One
tenant described her concern with security in this way.

Mrs. A.: They (the tenants of High Heaven) are afraid to go out.

Dr. J.: Are they afraid their purse will be snatched or what?

Mrs. A.: Well, there was a bunch of them (black girls) on day.
They were going to — this was before I had my heart
operation — there was about ten of them waiting for a
bus and they said, "Here comes this white lady, let's get

her," or something (like that). And I had my purse, and I said to them, this one girl says, "let's get her." I said, "Well you hadn't better try, you'll be sorry." I said, "I'm not afraid just because you're in a gang." But I let her know I wasn't scared. I got in my car, I always lock my car the minute I get in. You know, they just walked away. Now, they could have (robbed me). What chance would've I had with about eight of them girls. . . . I said, "Well you hadn't better try." I don't always carry my purse and I never carry much money. The only thing I was worried was losing my drivers license. Losing that, because they put you through so much red tape to get it back. Well, quite a few women have had their pocketbooks taken. And one lady in here, she has to walk with a cane, and they attacked her twice. But what she does, she gets out of her car backwards. They were probably hiding by the trees. And she always carries money with her. I've told her many time, I said, "Molly, I wouldn't do that, and I wouldn't get out backwards." She said, "I have to," on account of they knocked her down one day and she broke her hip. She was in the hospital for quite a while. A person like her, they probably know her; they've got her number, and she shouldn't come home late at night. But when I went out before I always came home at a certain time and then I didn't go out again. . . . It could be anyone. If you're going to your car, you're getting out of your car, they're hiding behind other cars, and you wouldn't see them, you know. But if I see anybody, now like when I would come home, like before when I went with this friend of mine (a male resident at High Heaven), I used to go play bingo. When I would come home it would be maybe 10:30, but I would drive around and if I see anybody loitering or anybody around here, I would just ride around. One time I rode around and I went on down and there was a policemen sitting in a car inside the underpass down there, you know. I pulled up there, and I said, "Officer, there's some young fellows loitering around those cars and I've got to get out of my car," I said, "Would you follow me?" He said, "I sure would." If I see them, I wouldn't get out. Another time I came home, and this man lives here was with three college boys from the college, and there was some fellows, colored, loitering around in the parking lot. So he came up to me and he said to me, "Don't worry, I'm watching you. Get out of your car." And I went up in there and he was with three college boys. These fellows were down there, and after I got into there (High Heaven) I watched and he and the (college boys went up to these fellows, and I don't know what happened — I came upstairs, I didn't bother (to wait and see). But I was fortunate that time. But if I see them I wouldn't get out of the car.... I think they should have a security guard twenty-four hours a day because it really isn't safe. They're (the tenants) really afraid. Sometimes they go down to pay their rent (at the housing office one block away), they'd be approached by somebody. I think it would be nice if they had a place right in the building where you could pay your rent.

The residents' assessment of the extent of the security problem has led many to become shut-ins. They were reluctant to leave the building unaccompanied, day or night. This orientation to their environment has of course had a stifling effect upon their social life. For example, the university provides for students and the public free or inexpensive film series on campus, not to mention free access to university classes for the residents. There are no residents who avail themselves of these services since it requires that they go out in the evening to gain access to them. Some will not walk the fifty yards or so to the student dining hall for a meal unchaperoned for fear of attack, while others who used to enjoy walking in the neighborhood during the daylight hours refrain from such activity and stay sequestered within the building.

This is particularly distressing since the residents have a potential interest in films and classes. This can be seen by the fact that the student-sponsored film series (now discontinued) formerly held within High Heaven was well-attended. A substitute travelogue film series established by the resident librarian is still well-attended. A recent class on the aged presented in High Heaven by the school of social work was also well-attended. What is needed is to bring these activities to the residents or provide transportation and other incentives to bring the residents to the activities. In any case, security, or the lack of it as the residents see it, has badly restricted their level of social involvement. The blame for this has fallen primarily upon the housing authority who, the residents feel, is unable or unwilling to provide them with full-time security personnel. This, too, has done little to endear the housing authority to the residents.

Another problem that has led to resident isolation and resentment toward the housing authority (and also contributed to the lessening of resident-student interaction) is the changing population of the residents themselves. The resident population has within the past couple of years become older and less self-sufficient. The initial conception of high Heaven as a facility for the well-elderly has, in practice, been all but abandoned. This is true not only because the initial cohort has become older and more infirm, but because the tenant replacement policies of the housing authority (and the public health service who screens potential tenants) have been to admit older persons with lower capabilities. This in turn has had a demoralizing effect upon the remaining members of the initial cohort as well as upon High Heaven's more recent and more able residents. It has also required them to act, more often than was previously the case, as helping agents to sickly neighbors. While the self-esteem of some residents was enhanced by these good works, many others felt it a great imposition, one that required a greater effort than they were either able or willing to expend. They felt that High Heaven should serve persons who are capable of caring for themselves, a condition of admission for the initial cohort, or that if a limited number of less able persons are allowed to live there, the housing authority, public health service or other agencies should provide for their care. Finally, this trend has been accentuated by the reluctance of the housing authority and the residents themselves to transfer aging and infirm tenants to nursing homes or the care of relatives or other concerned parties. There have been very few evictions from High Heaven. One resident noted,

> Now, we have a woman on the first floor that brought it up
> yesterday. I don't know why in the world they'd rent an
> apartment to someone like that. First thing you know, they'll be
> renting an apartment to someone who's wanted (by the police).
> They just never check on things like that. It could be public
> enemy number 1. They don't check on these people well
> enough. Someone caught a woman going to the incinerator in
> the nude. She started yelling "Help me! help me! They are
> trying to kill me!" She gets the people all excited. She lives on
> (the ninth floor) and at 3:00 a.m. in the morning she was
> pushing everyone's doorbell. . . . How can they rent to people
> like that? We have people here in housing (in the housing
> authority) who said that they would take care of people like
> that. I contacted this woman who contacted (housing,
> to) . . . evict two individuals. It took us two years to get her
> committed to an institution.

Still another contributing factor to the lessening of student-
resident interaction generated during the golden era was the
elimination of the snack bar. This occurred in stages. First, the
maintenance of the snack bar and the facility housing it became
lax; then it was open only intermittently and at inconvenient
hours, and most recently it has closed down completely. This
space has since been allocated to the school of social work and the
snack bar and what it has formerly offered to the students and
residents of High Heaven has been eliminated.

What of the pot luck dinners, informal get-togethers and other
forms of student-resident interaction that were outlined earlier?
As things currently stand, there is very little interaction between
students and residents in these areas. Residents are never seen in
the dormitories even though these are located not more than one
hundred yards from High Heaven, and there are not more than six
or eight students who are now actively involved in the matching
program. During the height of activity there were at least four
times that number involved.

Some indication of how difficult it was for meaningful
interactions to occur between residents and students, even when
both parties were willing can be had from the following verbatim
accounts taken from a student's diary. Both student (Cathy

Comstock) and resident has recently volunteered to be a part of a match.

First visit:

> I called Mrs. O. and asked if I could come down the following day. She replied, "Yes, but not until 2:00."
>
> I arrived at Mrs. O's apartment an hour early, but I rang the doorbell anyway. No answer, so I went and sat in the floor lounge and sleepily stared at some plastic flowers. I wasn't really up for visiting, but felt an obligation. A few minutes went by and I got up to ring the bell again.
>
> From the peephole I could see someone coming. The door opened a smidgen and a fluffy, thin, white-haired head stuck out. I explained who I was and she welcomed me in with an eager grin. She had very few, very few wrinkles. I followed her to the living room.
>
> She was wearing just a thin blue, black and white bathrobe, unbuttoned, which after she took her seat, she buttoned and continued to unbutton. (Not for exhibition sake, I'm positive.) During my stay, her entire body was revealed to me. She had no hair aside that upon her head and her brows. I don't think she undid her robe due to nervousness (although there was not once eye contact on her behalf), but rather because of heat. She complained heavily of the heat. She had two fans, both of which were not functioning.
>
> The first thing I noticed was her feet. They were huge; her legs, grand; her thighs mammoth. Her toes were all criss-crossed. There seemed to be more than five on both feet. I stole several short stares, but still am unsure of the number. Does it matter? She tried to hide her swollen parts behind a big leather stool by tugging down her bathrobe. She told me immediately that she has water of the feet, water of the body, and that she was embarrassed. The excess water was due to her weight, but she had lost ten pounds and is still on a diet. She added that if she ate grossly, she would die. She had at least seven types of pills — her "life savers" — and a pill schedule which she seemed to regulate her life by. She dwelled on her sickness. "Old people get it all." Mrs. O. was extremely aware of her older age, but still full of laughter, mostly a sarcastic, knowing laughter.
>
> The TV was on loud and it interfered with our discussion. She kept mentioning that it should be switched off, but when her eyes were in need of contact the TV was where they seemed to

go, so I didn't offer to turn it off. I was half into what she was
saying and half into the drone of the soap operas. Her constant
talking and dwelling on sickness was pissing me off. She was
smiling, and I would force a grin. My plastic attitude was
annoying me also. In addition to the shouting of the TV, High
Heaven is situated on the highway so the zooming and speeding
of trucks and cars is constant. I was wondering if Mrs. O. was
trying to drown out the traffic with the TV. If so, she failed —
the noise was chaotic.

We discussed (she discussed) numerous things. She speed-
rapped. She was bright, and a free and easy talker....

While I was there, we ate. She offered me anything in her ice
box and I had a cucumber, some grapes and chocolate mints.
She had Spam, a tomato, a cucumber and grapes. She ate with a
knife and used the knife to enforce her words. We touched water
glasses and made a toast to water because she likes it. Her diet is
mainly vegetables and she wants everything she can't have.
Afterwards, I helped her clean up. She is extremely appreciative
and receptive to people helping her. She mentioned all the
things she would cook me. She is generous and willing.

Her apartment was a mess — filth all over. This was because
she had difficulty moving. She has a cleaning lady come once a
month. Her bed gets changed then.

I asked Mrs. O. if she would play bingo with me some night,
and I was surprised to hear her say yes, but only if I went.

She was sad to see me go. She walked me to the door which
was difficult for her — watching me disappear.

I met a kind soul today, a lonely soul.

Second visit:

A nice day. Little breeze, but not hot. Walking
weather/sitting weather. Definitely a time to be out-of-doors.
The lobby of High Heaven was people-packed. Appearances
were disturbing, beast-like, ugly features unavoidable. One lady
caught my eye. Her chin appeared to be stuck to her neck. She
dared not look up. Her head was bent, stuck bent to a glued
position of uncomfort. She reminded me of a character from a
short story who was hunger-starved. His head was bent also so
that his chin screwed and screwed, driving his bone deep into
his neck. He was in need of food; the lady was love-starved.

One characteristic of all the aged is love-starvation. Everyone
desires love, but the aged feel it more. The end of their life is

near.

I arrived at Mrs. O's hoping that she would go outside with me, but no. She was having trouble moving she said, but was moving more than the previous day. She said she had no energy. She also did not want to go outside because she felt that it is only respectful to be seen in public well-dressed, and it is a pain for her to get dressed up. So I sat down on a couch opposite her (my place) and we talked. I turned off the TV first. The room was still noisy, the loudness of traffic was incredible, but I could listen and I did. It was her granddaughter's birthday so I suggested that *we* bake a cake. "O.K.," she replied. I ended up cooking the entire thing. I didn't mind. It smelled good and she thought so too because she thought that we should eat it. I refused and she said she'd save it for me. I inquired about her granddaughter's birthday and she replied that she was giving her money anyway. This irritated me; her entire motive was sneaky. Mrs. O wanted me to cut the cake so that she could have a piece. I'd be doing the dirty work so that she wouldn't feel guilty. She also wanted to eat the cake in revenge, feeling that her daughter didn't love her, so she wouldn't give her the cake, but she'd only give her money instead. I left with the cake untouched.

I met her daughter, Jane, who came over for about an hour and knitted and talked little. They were amazingly similar. Both, when they talked, did so at the same time. Neither would halt for the other's voice to be heard. It was like a competition, then silence. Jane was not very warm. She ate and ran and left her mess. I did her dishes, plus everything else that was piled about.

I didn't realize it until too late but Mrs. O. was using me to do her work. At one point she offered me money. I refused. There was a tiny argument over money. I didn't know if she wanted me to have it because (1) she knew I was broke, (2) for doing her chores, or (3) for being her friend. Whatever it was, I will never take money.

Not only did I bake her a cake, but she sent me to the lobby to get her mail. I should have said no, but I thought too late. She does not like to venture out. I am learning. She will learn.

Mrs. O. was moody today. She seemed sad. I wanted to help her arise from the pit — I was angry for her blindness. This is going to be a long, involved relationship. I just realized that I was subtly planning to mold her to what I think is best — missionary instinct.

No, honestly I do not wish to mold her. I just want her to hear what I have to say, and to feel what I have to give. I want her to know people interacting in a reciprocal bond is necessary, and that will give love, life and time to a person. She hates people and the outdoors — I am opposite. There is tension in our discussion. She loves to play tricks on people, especially the old; she mocks them. Her humor is in the garbage can. She plays cruel tricks to inflict pain. I told her what she was doing with her little games, and she said, "Oh, you think I am awful."

Laughing, I said, "Yes".

Another indication of the current lack of interaction between students and residents can be seen from how few tenants now share the dining facilities with the students (usually none at breakfast, two or three at lunch, and not more than a dozen at the dinner hour). Even these few tend to congregate in a group off by themselves and have very little if any direct contact with students.

There is still occasional contact between students and residents at holiday get togethers, e.g. Halloween, Thanksgiving and Christmas parties. However, these occur two or three times a year, and while they usually involve a relatively large number of residents, they rarely draw more than two or three students. An example of this was the Thanksgiving dinner that High Heaven held for residents and students. While the resident turnout was good, perhaps the best in High Heaven's history — about 120 persons, the only students present were the dorm representative, whose job it was to represent the students and encourage their participation; a friend who was not a student who had come to visit her over the holiday; and a student of the author's from a gerontology class who attended as part of an assignment.

Another indicator of student-resident apathy was an effort on the part of at least some residents (a survey revealed that enthusiasm was not widespread) to revive the High Heaven weekly newsletter that had become defunct about two years ago. It had formerly been put out by the residents with assistance from a student during the golden era. The problem was to get the university or some other agency to donate two or three hundred dollars for material, get resident volunteers to put the newsletter together, and enlist the aid of a journalism student to assist in the enterprise. With time the university did pledge its support by way of donating the money for supplies, but thus far the resident and student volunteers have not materialized; neither has the newsletter.

The elimination of the student-resident snack bar was noted previously. More recently other efforts have been made to make incursions into the residents' social space. The school of law, looking for an appropriate location for a community legal aid office for older persons, thought that High Heaven would be a good choice. A general meeting of the residents was held where a law professor outlined the proposed legal aid office and how it would benefit the community and the residents. A resident vote was taken and the project was overwhelmingly rejected. (The residents had not had a vote on what was to become of the snack bar since this was in a university facility, and not a part of High Heaven proper.)

The following edited transcribed verbatim account will give some flavor of the proceedings and the gulf that existed between the tenants and the law school representative.

Mr. B. (the law school representative): I think it important for you to know the nature of our program, and it's not only because of the possibility we might want to use space in High Heaven to house our program, but also because our program is designed specifically to help older people in the area with their legal problems. The university received a grant from a foundation in New York City, and the purpose of the grant was expressly to create a program that would serve older people in (this area) with legal services for no charge, and that is what we do. . . . I have approximately one dozen law students who work with me in our supervised (program) and we have, in addition, graduate students in social work who work in the program, and our only function is to serve you and others like you. So that means if you have a problem with Social Security, for example, or Medicare, if you want a will drawn, if you have received something from Social Security, probably, and don't

understand what the letter says...for you to do, our
purpose is to be there to serve you. Right now our office
is located in the gerontology center directly across from
the plaza from the entrance to High Heaven. We can't
occupy that space more than on a temporary basis and
are trying to find a location that will be suitable for our
office to be located in. We want to find a place that
people know about and can get to, so one place that fits
that description is High Heaven. People know about
High Heaven. All of you live here, and there are people
who live down at (another housing authority facility)
which is nearby, and so we thought, if it was possible,
we would like to work out an arrangement with the
housing authority and, if we could, locate our office in
this building. Now, if we do locate the office in the
building, the space that we're talking about is the two
offices in the left rear of the ground floor to the left of
the elevator that is not Kenneth's office. Now, we might
be able to share with Mr. T, or we might work an
arrangement under which he would move to another
location in the building. We would also use, if your
permission is granted, approximately one-third of
what is now the drop-in center. That is, that area that
covers the drop-in center and to the right of you as you
walk in the door. We're not talking about that whole
room, just that section to the right. What we would
probably do is throw up some sort of a wall, and then
make offices there so that people could come to us and
talk about their private legal problems in private.
That's the thing that we're interested in is having an
office, a private office that everyone can come to and
feel comfortable (in) and talk about their private
problems in. So, I guess the best thing for me to do is
ask if anyone has questions about our office and about
our plan, our desire to locate here....And I guess I've
implied but hadn't said explicitly that our program
will serve not just people in High Heaven, but all older
people in the area, so there would be people coming

into the building during office hours, from nine to five on weekdays, and so that people like yourselves who happen to live somewhere else could come in to use our office when they needed some help. So, is there any questions? I'd be very happy to answer them, both about our services and our program. Wherever our program ends up, our only purpose is to serve people like yourselves with their legal problems.

Mr. R. (Resident council president): Does anyone have any questions they want to ask Mr. B.?

Mrs. F.: I want to ask Mr. B., in all due respects.... What about the cafeteria (as a place to relocate legal aid) for the past year....

Mr. B.: We're presently located in what has been the delicatessen. Now that office, the university simply. ... We're investigating that possibility, but right now it looks like the university is going to use that space to put the university offices in, and so that space will not be available to us on more than a temporary basis.

Mrs. F.: The university has enought property here.... And I'm not only speaking for myself (but) for a lot of people who have suggested to me.... and I say that that (the drop-in room) is where tenants go to sit down and relax and you can't very well do it if classes are being held in the other room.

Mr. B.: No classes are going to be taught here. Now, what we're talking about is a law office. A law office that will serve you without fee.

Mrs. F.: We've had that.... for the last three years, but we have been coming up on Wednesday nights to see the lawyers....And that was all for free, too. The part is that they will take over part of the terrace (floor where social events are currently staged).

Mrs. Y.: I think that the program is very worthwhile. The question in my mind is opening the doors.... I don't feel that I'm secure. The question is about opening the doors for so many coming in from everywhere.

Mr. B.: All right let me tell you. I recognize that problem, and this is to explain the way our office works. We have a flyer that I think that most of you receive describing our offices. The way we operate is that the person who has a problem telephones our office and makes an appointment with us. Someone outside the building would telephone us and we would schedule an appointment with them for the following day or etc. We would then know who is coming and when they are coming in. There is then no concern about someone coming and abusing our services. They are then actually using our services. Our clients are people like yourselves, and you should not be worrying about some coming in on a frequent basis. Our offices are located... right by the doors. Security problems won't exist on a great scale.... If that's the concern, I would work out a system so that security is safe....

Mr. O.:   Every night there is people's playing every kind of game (in the drop-in room). There is always one bridge game. It's all right... but what are you going to do with them.

Mr. B.:   Are you saying that there would not be room for the people who play bridge games at night?

Mr. O.:   That's right.

Mr. B.:   Well, again, I don't know, but I think that that's the kind of problem that we can work out between ourselves and others. Let's see if some other combination can be reached. I can try to make arrangements so that your present activities are not interrupted. I don't make rules and regulations today, but if you vote for me I can certainly try to make arrangements.

Mr. X.:   Apparently you have had designs on this room for the past couple of weeks. You looked at the room and you have not seen very many people in there. At this time the weather is good and the people are outside. If you were to come at another time, you would see many and a variety of tenants. Some want to get out of their rooms and like to come downstairs, find a chair and set in a corner. They may never talk to anyone, but they still like to get out of their efficiency apartments. Then there is others who get together, tell stories, play bridge and play pinochle. If you were to come here a little later in the season, I would feel that you would see that there is a definite need for this room. I'm not trying to say that you're not trying to help, but I feel that those tenants who cannot get out (of High Heaven) the way I do need that room. I think that it would be an injustice to take it away from them. (Clapping)

Mr. B.:   I'm aware that you have other things planned. It seems to me that this is a big enough building, and that you could do all the things that you like to do without any interference. And with the addition of a legal office to aid you....

Miss H. (a High Heaven tenant): I want to say the service that they want to provide is fine. I was associated with OCES, and I had to plead with the people to come with legal problems. The office had a lawyer, secretary and everything else, but they still wouldn't come down. The proposed office would be very disappointed to know that the people don't want that much legal attention.

In keeping with the contention of the last speaker is the fact that nowhere in the entire transcript (edited portions of which appear here) was there any question by the tenants directed to the nature of services Mr. B.'s program promised to deliver. Indeed, there was little interest in the program itself by the residents and much apprehension. The law school was of course disappointed at the loss of a potential site and could not understand why the residents voted against receiving free legal aid, something the law school was sure many older persons required and could ill afford. The residents of course held another view. First and foremost was the fact that the services to be offered were not exclusively for the residents of High Heaven, but for members of the neighboring community as well. These were defined as potential enemies by the residents, and they viewed their coming and going in the building in pursuit of legal aid as aggravating an already bad security situation. Secondly, establishing the legal aid office in High Heaven would require that the residents relinquish some of the area they now used for social activities. There was a strong sentiment against that as well. Finally, the residents' definition of the situation was that they rarely required legal services, and if they did, they would acquire it elsewhere. Some validation of this sentiment was obtained when a member of the law school enlisted the aid of a member of the resident research committee to canvas High Heaven residents in order to find, or interest them in seeking, the services that the legal aid office had to offer. After two weeks of concerted effort he was unable to find a single resident who expressed an interest in the services the law school offered.

OTHER CONTRIBUTING FACTORS

The early initiation by the university of student-resident programs designed to break down intergenerational differences has been discussed. Unfortunately, many of the differences that existed between students and residents were not age-related, e.g. educational achievement, family income, prior place of residence, social class background, etc. It was noted that in spite of this and other initial handicaps, a promising start was made toward fulfilling the project's early expectations. However, due to many unforeseen problems, some of which were outlined above, these early gains have for the most part been negated. As things now stand there is little direct interaction between the residents of High Heaven and the university students. In fact, many students are literally unaware that retired persons live in High Heaven or that there is or ever was any affiliation between the residents and students. Most students are neutral to the presence of the limited number of residents in the student dining hall and some are puzzled; others are openly hostile. This is not to say that students do not from time to time help residents with their trays or show them other courtesies; they do, but the overall picture is one of indifference and clanishness, both on the part of students and residents. Each group stays very much to itself even when in the other's presence.

However if most students would not miss the residents, many residents would miss the students. While the residents have little or no direct contact with the students, they are glad to see them everywhere and miss them during their absence, e.g. during holiday vacations. Residents talk of how dead it seems when the students leave, not because they have lost any direct link with them, but rather because of the barrenness of their environment without the students. Students are also considered if not friends, then at least not enemies. This is in marked contrast with how residents define the members of the adjacent black ghetto. As a result, some residents view the students as a buffer between them and ghetto residents. In brief, the residents are, by and large, much more favorably disposed toward the students than the students are toward them. They are aware of their different backgrounds, ideologies and expectations, but would like to have a greater, if limited involvement with students. As indicated earlier, those residents who were part of the initial cohort speak of the height of student-resident interaction as the golden era. Students and others who helped organize and realize these interactions, especially the dean of the school of social work and the original program coordinator, are referred to as folk heroes. Some, but by no means all residents, would like to return to these promising beginnings, but feel that there is very little hope. Some indication of this sentiment follows.

Dr. J.:   What about this? Student interaction is supposed to be part of the uniqueness of this setting. I don't see many students around here.

Mrs. B. (one of the first tenants to occupy High Heaven): I don't either. Personally, I have never been approached or involved in any way with any of the students. I never knew that much about that. I think it would be absolutly great, I'm not against it; I think it would be beautiful. It doesn't seem to be very (likely though). . . . I have never known one instance, not even one instance where a student was involved.

Dr. J.:   Do you think other people think like you do — that they would like (more student involvement), but it just didn't happen — like they would like to see students? Or do you think some would rather not see students?

Mrs. B.: No, I think most everybody would be interested. I don't know how the ball would get rolling. I don't know (what) you would do to get it going. I have no idea.

Dr. J.: But if — but apart from the mechanics of it — if it could happen somehow, do you think people would like it?

Mrs. B.: Yeh. I don't see where it would help the students, I really can't.

Dr. J.: You just think it would help the residents more, and not the students very much?

Mrs. B.: Because I think perhaps a lot of these older people are stagnating, and I think they would enjoy being pepped up a little bit. You really can stagnate. There are a lot of people in this building who really and truly just keep to themselves. A lot of them are ill and, let's face it, a lot of them are antisocial. A lot of them are bitter with life and I do think the ones that keep to their apartment (if they are not ill), I think they are bitter; I think they are brooders — they brood a lot about themselves mainly. That's really too bad, but retirement is hard for a lot of people to take. I love it myself. I've only had a year of it, but I guess it makes a difference — I am able to go back to work, and I know if I wanted to, I could go back to work. If I was eighty and knew I could never, the way they look at it, do anything useful again, that might be very depressing. It probably is to a lot of these people.

Mrs. B. feels that the residents could gain much from student interaction while the students would gain little. Another resident felt the students would probably benefit most.

Mrs. O.: Mrs. L. and I talked this over many times. We feel that we could help these students because some of them are coming in as freshmen. Now if she (some freshman she knew of) had somebody to go to, maybe, and unburden her troubles to, and feel that she is back in familiar territory again, people that are kind of settled like some of the students are far out, you know (she might feel much better). . . . We (she and the students she has had contact with) talk about everything, and I just think the students (are great). I don't see any generation gap. Now here's what; some students would come from a home, maybe where the parents are maybe in their forties, and they're very busy with thier own life and making a lot of money and so on, and maybe the students haven't had grandparents or wanted to talk to somebody who has lived a little longer. Now we should be acting as substitute parents and grandparents, uncles and what have you, and I think that is what we should be doing. I think it is our duty to do it. How can you pass an opportunity by? Maybe these students need us over there and we are here. Now everybody in this building doesn't feel like I feel, (but) this is how a lot of us feel. How it can be done, I don't know.

Mr. R. (a third resident): Most of the people like to see the kids (the students) around. They miss them (during vacations). They are glad to see them when they come back. Most of them are friendly and cooperative together. We have a Halloween party together. Everyone enjoys that. We have a Christmas party together, and I think that there are one or two other little get-togethers that they help out on. Students get together and do all kinds of things. This Thanksgiving party dinner we had here last year — the students helped out on that. Matter of fact, they took a big part in that. It does make a difference (student-resident interaction). It's a tie-in.

The Thanksgiving party was the one referred to earlier. It's true the students did play a big part in making the party a success, but there were only two students involved. One, the dorm R.A., had an obligation to be there; the second, a student in the author's class, was there as part of a research project. In short, unless one were present at the party, it would be easy to misread the extent of student involvement. This was true of most of the residents' comments on the extent of student resident interaction.*

---

*It is possible not only to overestimate the extent of student involvement from the residents' accounts, but one may overestimate the extent of resident involvement. For example, the author learned that the High Heaven Bridge Club has about thirty active members (usually 7 tables, with 4 persons at each). Quite naturally he assumed that there were primarily resident bridge players at bridge club meetings, and perhaps a few students. Actually, the High Heaven Bridge Club membership is currently comprised of one resident of High Heaven and twenty-seven or twenty-eight university students and faculty. While this exceptional case indicates extensive student-faculty involvement with High Heaven (on one evening a week), it represents little or no interaction between the residents and students or faculty.

Another growing problem is that new residents, i.e. those not a part of the original cohort, are viewed by the established tenants as apathetic and unwilling to help, not only with resident-student projects, but with in-house projects as well. The feeling of the more active and involved residents is that everything has fallen on their shoulders, and that they have weakened with time and are no longer as enthusiastic or active as they used to be. What is needed, from their perspective, is a dynamic outside third party, an advocate such as the first coordinator of social services at High Heaven. Without such assistance, residents and students simply lapsed into their initial state of apathy and indifference. At the time of the study the sort of charismatic replacement the residents had in mind and the support program he or she would require were nowhere in sight.

LIFE AT HIGH HEAVEN

Such is the current state of resident-student interaction. What is the situation like with respect to the routine activities and states of mind of residents and students? Thus far, little has been said of what the residents do on a day-to-day basis or what they think of High Heaven or why.

Most residents at High Heaven (at least those in the original cohort) felt upon first coming there that there was much to be said in its favor. First and foremost in this regard was the fact that it offered better living accommodations than were available elsewhere. Indeed, given the background of some of the residents, High Heaven was viewed as offering luxury accommodations for very low rents. This evaluation has not changed. However, many things have changed in the past four years to cause them to reassess its desirability. The following is a transcribed account from an interview with the former training director of social work students during the golden era who has recently been conducting a series of observations at High Heaven. He points up a number of before and after distinctions.

Dr. J.:   What are some of your impressions regarding the before and after at High Heaven? What do you see now that you didn't see then (during the golden era), or what don't you see now that you did see then?

Director: ... There is just not the activity downstairs (on the first floor) that there used to be. There used to be a good deal of activity. As I reminisce here, the director (of social services) had his desk right in the social hall and his secretary (was there also).... and, because he was popular, they (the students) were down there (as well), and there was always a lot of interaction as a result of that. The new director (the one appointed by the housing authority) has her office in the back in a room that is separate from the main area so she is more or less hidden from view. (It might be added that her time is split between High Heaven and the other housing authority facilities so that she spends relatively little time there compared with the initial director of social services, and, more important, she does not live at High Heaven as the original director did). So, what I saw was a decrease in activity and interaction on the main floor, more people with physical handicaps than I had seen before and more black faces. I think that those three factors struck me most.

These and other factors will be dealt with in some detail in the following pages.

Race and Racism

While there are not many black residents in High Heaven (there are currently about 24 out of a total of 420 residents), there are more now than there used to be, and many more than some of the early residents had expected. Indeed, some has initially thought that High Heaven was exclusively for whites. Since blacks are associated in the minds of many residents with feelings of insecurity, and since influential persons on key resident committees within High Heaven are openly racist and aggravate this condition, some residents have been led to re-evaluate the desirability of High Heaven as a retirement setting.

The following is an example that illustrates the racist and ethnic resentment that some residents bare toward each other. It is taken from one of the transcribed, tape-recorded interviews.

Dr. J.: How long have you lived here?

Mr. H.: '69.

Dr. J.:   Since 1969?

Mr. H.: Right, we were the first ones. The whole damn place was all white (there were no black residents at the time) ... Well, we had to get out of there (their last apartment in a different public housing project) because of my heart. I had a sickness over in the other housing project. They had an upstairs. ... up and down stairs every time you had to go to the bathroom... (I had) a long wait trying to get in here.

Dr. J.:   How long did it take you to get into High Heaven?

Mr. H.: Two years. We had a fight. Had to get the colored bunch over there. They (the blacks) are backed by the government now... They got in here right away — on their months notice. ... a lot of them in here right now shouldn't be. (Some of them) that's got a lot of money in the Goddamn bank and safe deposit box on this floor here (that live on this floor). ... that one over there is a Jewish family. I don't know what you are, Jewish or what. You Jewish?

Dr. J.:   Yes, I am.

Mr. H.: You are, well I'm talking right from the shoulder, I'm not throwing no Goddamn punches. They (the Jews) were running the Goddamn place (High Heaven) when it first opened up. ...

In the first few minutes of the interview, Mr. H. had managed to malign the blacks, the Jews, the government and those who possessed (he thought) more money than was allowed under the financial need entrance requirement clause for public housing. An interesting postscript to the above was the fact that Mr. H., who was not rich, black, Jewish or a government employee, was the current president of one of the key in-house resident committees, and had been very influential in remaking it in his image.

Mr. R. (another resident, a member of another key in-house committee): ... and another thing too, you are going to have the same problems of (black) kids coming into this building. Ask them where they are going and they say that they are going to see their grandfather. They are running around the hallways. Kids have been found in apartments. When they go up to Northside, you are going to attract kids up there. It's going to be the same things. It's going to be hard to walk from the front entrance to the building to the parking lot. What they (the housing authority and government) are doing is forcing us (blacks and whites) together. Let nature take its course. Our lives come to end and the world still goes on. But see, what they (the blacks) want is now; they want to get everything together. They want it NOW. See what I mean, they want it TODAY; they don't want to wait until TOMORROW. Every time you get up and talk about things, they always yell about housing. They (the blacks) don't care what they live in. Give them a bale of straw down south (like) these (black) migrant workers had; (that) is all they know. And here (in the north), I mean that they don't want that. They keep pushing for more and ruin everything. Did you see what they did to the Southside? Did you see what they (the young blacks) did to the university co-eds? These co-eds are getting raped right and left, but they don't report it. Just like a policeman told me, if you knew what was going on, we'd be at war with these blacks. We'd take everything from them, everything. My complaint is that they don't appreciate or don't seem to protect public housing. The ones (the blacks) we have in this building — the Senior Citizens — most of them are good people. Most of them want you to know that they are immaculate. When they clean, they are extra clean, but you know, it's their children that are the ones that are not happy. They want this, and they want better jobs, white collar jobs and higher pay — all that. But you see, (when) this generation (of blacks) are gone...(they are nice people; you can live with them) when this other generation (of blacks) comes up (the younger generation), they are bitter people. They are bitter at what happened 300 years ago.... See what I mean, they want to take it out on us. It is going to hurt us when these people (the older blacks) die off. This morning I looked at a car, and someone took a screwdriver and put a lot of nice marks on it. I don't know who did it, but it had to happen here. I'm not sure what happened, but I have my own ideas on it. I'm not the only one. There has been thousands of dollars worth of damage done in the parking lot. They had no business building this housing where they did. We don't know what the government had in mind. It's a complex. I think what they should do is move us the hell out of here without delay and turn this place over to the university for married couples. They (the university) need space so bad. They just built space. It's part of the university and I think that the government has been making some arrangements. At the end of a period of time it (High Heaven should) go to the university. They took an interest in us. But....

Dr. J.: Do you think that the tenants who like the students... that they would give that up if they could get into a different place?

Mr. R.: Definitely. We are in the wrong location. There's that Jones Square (another nearby public housing facility occupied almost exclusively by blacks). We hear guns going off (there), and there are all kinds of murders in the paper. Just down here two blocks on Jones Street, right here in back of this (building) they found a man dead. Let us retire with dignity. This place (High Heaven) is mislocated. It shouldn't have been here....

Well, I didn't know about these racial problems out here. (He formerly resided in another state.) No one told me about them, and I came here cold turkey. No one told me about them problems — riots and all that. When I left here (some years before) there were about 3,000 strong, and now (upon his return) there are about 23,000 strong. Now don't misunderstand me, we are not condemning black people. When I was young, they were wonderful people. (Black) people in this building are wonderful people. I think you understand thoroughly and exactly what I mean. It's these ones that go out and (you) can't please. If you don't believe me, turn the TV on. Channel 24 has all blacks. They are always fighting for something and can never be pleased. They are never satisfied.

Dr. J.: Then it's the younger generation of blacks that you think are...

Mr. R.: The older generation are wonderful people. They are always very happy, and the white people always liked them, and the younger generation is the ones that hate the white. They hate us more than we hate them. I'm not speaking about my age bracket. It's the college scene. In the colleges they teach them different; they are forcing them together. They should not be forcing them together. They are starting in grammar school. Hold hands. Start raising them up together and they don't know that there is a difference. There is a difference ...

Dr. J. (A third resident): Do you think there is any ill feelings? Well, you know there are some black people in the building, there are some Jewish people in the building...

Mr. B.: (A third resident): That is one thing we didn't quite — didn't think when we came in here (High Heaven) — that there would be so many colored people as there is; there is quite a few of them in here and more coming all the time. Some of them are wonderful, just like our own people. Some that are not so good.

Dr. J.: But it's something you didn't figure on in any case when you first moved in — you didn't know that...

Mr. B.: Oh no, no. Never gave it a thought. They are all right, they've got to live, they've got to be taken care of the same as everybody else. When they get into a place like this — maybe I shouldn't say this —

Dr. J.: No, you speak your mind.

Mr. B.: They've got an independent attitude — I'm here, the heck with you, Jack. That don't go over. People resent that, and I've heard a lot of people say that. They are pushy, you know — I'm black I'm going and that's the way it is. But as a whole, they are — we have some very nice colored people.

Dr. J.: Do you think some people who didn't figure on blacks would have preferred to have different neighbors?

Mr. B.: That's right, that's for sure.

Dr. J.: How about the Jewish people?

Mr. B.: Oh well, they mix good, they mix good. We get a lot of Jewish people in here — we haven't got — let's see, we've got four on this floor. They are wonderful people. Wonderful.

Dr. J.: So there is some reservation about blacks, but not the Jewish people?

Mr. B.: Not the Jewish people. That, they (the residents) kind of draw the line on (that) — that's for sure.

While the author encountered what was patently racist comments from some residents, he does not intend the reader to infer that all of the residents of High Heaven were racists — they were not. However, many holding key in-house office positions on resident committees, such as those noted above, were racists, and, as opinion leaders, served to influence the attitudes and actions of more neutral residents. As a result of this (and other factors), many residents would prefer, given the option, to move to new retirement settings being built in the area, insofar as they were viewed as being located in better neighborhoods, i.e. further from the black ghetto.

Other concerns have developed that have caused many residents to reevaluate their early and more favorable impressions of High Heaven. Some of these have already been noted. One important factor in this growing list of discontents is the original cohort's disenchantment with expanding resident apathy. Some indication of the extent that this has reached is that chairmen of resident committees are no longer elected or appointed — they are captured. No one wants to become a committee member, and some in-house clubs and committees are threatened with extinction. This, again, is in sharp contrast to the good old days of greater resident-student involvement.

Dr. J.: What kinds of things do you do around....

Mrs. A.: Around the building? Well, Mondays I have meals on wheels — you know, (I) deliver meals (to those residents of High Heaven who are recuperating from a serious illness or are otherwise incapable of preparing their own meals. There are currently about fifteen residents receiving meals on wheels.) Like today, I helped another one. This other woman — we've had it (meals on wheels) for nearly four years on Mondays, and then we play bingo friday nights. Monday night is game night, and we all go down and play pinochle. Then we play pinochle maybe, (with) this one woman, Anny (a friend of hers). Well we get together and play any night during the week that we can get a game — to play. That's all. Go downtown and gad around. Not much of anything you can do.

Dr. J.: Do you visit each other?

Mrs. A.: Oh, not too much. We did at first (during the golden era), but there's a different bunch in here now than was. When we first moved in everybody was together.

Dr. J.: Is that so?

Mrs. A.: Now it's fallen off.

Dr. J.: How come?

Mrs. A.: Different people.

Dr. J.: Just different people move in and...

Mrs. A.: They are a different class entirely. I don't understand it. We used to have dances and parties and everything. Now, nothing. They just don't want to get together. Even the students, I mean, we had a group going together with the students and us. They have now, they've started again, but it's not the same. This bunch, we were always back and forth (students and residents visiting each other). We used to have parties, a lot of parties, but now that bunch (of residents) is gone and the new bunch don't seem to — they seem to be more for the money part of it, not the fun (students do odd jobs for residents for money). Like, they are having a big (bake) sale Sunday and it's the money — I don't know what they plan on doing for it.

Dr. J.: You mean the residents are more for the money?

Mrs. A.: No, the students. We do the baking for the sale — bake sale — and they say they put in (the money made at the bake sale) in a fund for parties, but there is only a couple of parties (a year); that's all.

Dr. J.: You mean the people in the building have a fund for parties, but they don't...

Mrs. A.: They put it together, students and tenants (of High Heaven). We do the baking for them, baking cakes and stuff and they (the students) sell it. The proceeds, we keep it together. I dropped out of it; I just don't seem to be interested in it no more.

Dr. J.: But they don't seem to have parties you think...

Mrs. A.: Not like we did.

Dr. J.: Do you think it's just different people or remember, Bruce T. (the original coordinator of social services at High Heaven) was around....

Mrs. A.: Oh, Bruce — he did. I'm telling you, Bruce kept things going. He sure did, Bruce and Mike (another member of the magnificent seven. I have quite a few pictures of the different groups that we had going (then).

Dr. J.: So it seems that there was quite a bit started between the students and the residents a couple of years ago.

Mrs. A.: When they first started out — groups, different things going. We really did a lot.

Dr. J.: Now it's different?

Mrs. A.: Right, The people don't seem to want to (participate); they hibernate I guess.

Dr. J.: You think the people were so different then?

Mrs. A.: It was the people; that's what I mean.

Dr. J.: It wasn't just who was here to organize it; it was more the people that were different?

Mrs. A.: Well, both.

Dr. J.: How were they different? What kinds of people were they?

Mrs. A.: There's a lot of colored in here too, now. I shouldn't say, but...

Dr. J.: No, you speak your mind. (Mrs. A. makes no further reference to the blacks at High Heaven and begins instead of talking of how certain tenants used to be active but no longer are.)

Mrs. A.: They (the residents of High Heaven) don't want to mix. They don't. There's a couple of them...The ones that were full of fun have died. There's quite a few of them...like Anny, she was able to get out of the wheelchair then. Now she's right to the chair; she can't move out if it. Different ones. Now there's Stella, she was always a lively one. She doesn't bother no more either. It may be they are getting older, I don't know. It could be that.

Dr. J.: So you get the feeling that a lot of people kind of stick to themselves in the building, more now than they used to?

Mrs. A.: Like, there's Bobbie, she died, and there's so many of them that were all in the group together — they are all dead. Stella can't see any more; she can't get around. There's so many of them — they are either sick or died. Stella, she's a nice girl; she's the life of the party always.

Dr. J.: So the people who first came to High Heaven knew each other as a group, then little by little some of the people just...

Mrs. A.: Drifted apart.

Dr. J.: Drifted apart. Then the people that drifted apart didn't make new friends? They just kind of stayed to themselves?

Mrs. A.: That's just the way it is.

Dr. J.: Do you think that's true for the people that came in later, like the newer people?

Mrs. A.: The new people don't associate at all, do they?

Mrs. R.: No, no they don't. They don't mix at all with us.

Dr. J.: Do they get together themselves?

Mrs. A.: I don't know. We don't see too much of them — the new people.

Mrs. R.: Since we've been here, we've seen a lot of them come and go. Some moved out. There was — some went in nursing homes and there are others that died.*

Dr. J.: What happened when there was a turnover in personnel, like Jill and Mr. T.? They were a kind of replacement for Bruce Thompson, weren't they?

Mrs. A.: I'm not going to say anything.

Dr. J.: You're not going to say anything?

---

*Some indication of the extent of tenant turnover at High Heaven can be obtained from the vital ststistics compiled by the housing authority on causes for moving out. The data indicate the following for the year 1972: deceased — 25; illness — 15; other — 12; over income — 0; eviction — 0. Of these, four were black; forty-eight, white; and zero, other.

Mrs. A.: No comments on that, no comments.

Dr. J.: Watever it is, it's between the three of us.

Mrs. A.: Sure ... They're (the new coordinators) in the office, and that's where they are and that's where they stay. The rest of us don't mean anything to them.

Dr. J.: You haven't seen much and they don't ... ?

Mrs. A.: They don't do nothing. You can't ask a question; they will evade it or they will, "I'll take it up later; I'll talk to you later, I'm busy now." Everything you say to them (they say) — "I'm busy, talk to you later." That's the way it goes in the office. As far as — Bruce was the best.

Changing Tenant Population

Finally many find the shift in resident population regarding the admittance and retention of less able residents demoralizing. It has in their opinion transformed High Heaven from a retirement setting into an old age home.

Mr. R.: You meet them half dead, and then you lose them. You see quite a few more deaths.

Dr. J.: Does that make it a little harder (to deal with death)?

Mr. R.: Yeah, you see you get that from living with people. They come in here half dead in the beginning. You have helped them and have done things for them and you get someone in here half dead. It has it advantages (living at High Heaven), and what are you going to do when you can't affort it (to go elsewhere)? Go out and live some place that is going to cost you $135.00 or $145.00 a month and, then, when the first of the year comes around, they want to raise your rent again every year.

Dr. J.: Do you think that most of the people who live in the building would if they were independently wealthy live in a place that has younger and healthier people around?

Mr. R.: No, I wouldn't live here unless I had to. ... I know a man in here, he was ninty-four years old and they took him out of a nursing home. They told him how to operate the showers and he was afraid to turn the handles because he might break them. I don't know. I was a little concerned about him. I thought that he might be a big nuisance, but he turned out to be a pretty good fellow. So far, he's holding up. But at ninety-four years old, what can you expect? They took him out of a nursing home and brought him in here. We're not able to take care of them people. All I can do is to take care of myself.

Dr. J.: Are there many people who are so sick that they can't get around much?

Mrs. S.: (another resident) We've got a lot of people like that. Oh yes, there's a lot of them. Fred was walking in here today. There's one fellow comes down today; he's in a wheelchair. He can't get to the store in the wheelchair and get in the store and get around the store in a wheelchair, so he has to have people in the lobby go get him things out of the store. Fred said one fellow come out of there and he asked him to bring back two six packs (of beer). He wouldn't settle for one; he wanted two.

Dr. J.: To tide him over, right?

Mr. S.: Save him a trip. No, there's quite a few people in here (who are disabled); in fact there's more of that type of people in here than I really thought when I was interviewed for the — this apartment. I didn't see this apartment before I came in because it wasn't ready. I didn't think there was going to be so many incapacitated people.

Dr. J.: So that was something you didn't figure on.

Mrs. S.: That's right. You know, it's a wonderful thing, God help them, they can't help it, but to go around one limping here, a walker here, a wheelchair here — it brings you down a little; you can't help it. That's for sure.*

---

*An analysis of data from the public health facility on the plaza floor indicates that they currently see about 150 residents of High Heaven as clients in one capacity or another. Of these, forty-eight use walkers or are in wheelchairs, fourteen use canes or crutches, twelve are blind or suffer from very poor vision, and another twenty-two are deaf or have moderate to severe hearing losses. Add to this numerous cases of diabetes, heart disease and high blood pressure, and one has a fair indication of the extent and nature of debilitating ailments suffered by the residents.

If the incapacities of others tended to be demoralizing and otherwise troublesome to some residents, the onset of their own serious physical illnesses frequently served to strengthen their bonds with their neighbors. This aspect will be considered in greater detail later. For the most part, however, residents tended to stay to themselves and pursue a life-style that may be characterized as *voluntary shut-in*. In short, many residents had little if any contact with their neighbors. This lack of contact and/or their low opinion of their neighbors stemmed from several different considerations.

Alcoholism

For example, drinking problems are prevalent in High Heaven. Some residents avoid the company of alcoholics or problem drinkers even though most drinking is done in private and causes little trouble for others. Some indication of the extent of alcoholism in High Heaven is given below.

Dr. J.: It sounds like there are drinking buddies, too (in High Heaven).

Mrs. B.: Oh yes, certainly.

Dr. J.: Friends that get together and socialize and drink together. Is there much of that, do you know?

Mrs. B.: Yes, yes, there's a lot of that. There's many alcoholics in this building.

Dr. J.: Well, everybody says, yeh, they take a friendly drink and so on. Some people are very reluctant to talk about drinking even though they know it's not the worst sin in the world.

Mrs. B.: Well, it's a sickness I guess. When you get to be an alcoholic, it's termed an illness. There are a lot of alcoholics in this building. I had to do with a lot of people when I was nursing (in High Heaven), and I know this for a fact — I know we've gotten in many, many apartments where we've had to search for bottles of booze, and it's a battle.

Dr. J.: How many would you guess, assuming there are 400 or so persons in the building, off the top of your head, would you term problem drinkers if not alcoholics?

Mrs. B.: I would think — oh . . . I think probably a quarter of the people at least, maybe more.

Mr. S.: (another resident) Well, there are some of those (heavy drinkers) in High Heaven. That's nothing unusual. There are a lot of those fellows who hang around down in the lobby down there; most all of those fellows do a little drinking. My neighbor over here will drink about 2 six packs a day.

Dr. J.: That's a fair amount of beer.

Mr. S.: He enjoys it. He doesn't get overloaded. I find that most of these people in here that do — well, there is a couple, I don't know them, but I've seen them; they've overdone it. But as a rule . . .

Dr. J.: The people that sit and drink by themselves don't make any trouble.

Mr. S.: That's right. About 90 percent of it is that way. You'd be surprised the number of women in here — don't go for the beer; they go for the hard stuff.

The Gossip Mill

There are a number of High Heaven residents who dislike blacks or Jews, or otherwise gossip indiscriminately about this or that facet of their neighbor's lives. In fact, the gossip mill plays a key role in High Heaven's social life.

Dr. J.: So you have the feeling that a lot of people spend a fair amount of time out of the building during the day.

Mrs. B. (a resident): Oh yes. This is a busy, busy place.

Dr. J.: And they don't go to the gossip room . . .?

Mrs. B.: Oh yes. Like I, they have a destination and they just go out the door and say hello as they go, and hello as they come in. Not to slight anyone, but a lot of people are not interested in sitting down there (in the gossip room). It's impossible. I don't know if it's older people, but it seems impossible for more than two people to sit down unless there is gossip.

Dr. J.: There doesn't seem to be many gossipers, at least in terms of the number of older people in the building. There aren't very many people down there often.

Mrs. B.: I think the drop-in lounge is the most popular (place in High Heaven), but it isn't as popular, either, as it used to be. A lot of the gossipers have died. I often think it's that (gossiping) that hurried them on their way. I don't mean that.

Dr. J.: Do they have little get-togethers?

Mrs. O.: (another resident): Yes, sometimes. And I'll say, "Who's coming? Will you come for coffee? Well, who's coming?" So they tell me and I say, "Well, I'd prefer not to go with her there, because I like to speak freely, and I can't speak freely because I don't think it will be kept quiet." I don't believe in malicious gossip; I don't indulge in that. But you don't want to watch every damn word you are saying; it makes me nervous. I'm nervous anyway. And, so, I don't go everywhere I'm asked to go. I don't invite everybody in here because once you've broken bread with somebody, to me it's some kind of a rite — have a meal with somebody, you like them pretty well, to to their house and accept their hospitality, you must like them pretty well. They meet down in the drop-in room (the gossip room), you know where that is down there, now it's a dismal room — overhead light, the glare, the hard chairs, unattractive scenery. I don't know why they don't go up in the terrace lounge or somewhere, in their own apartment, invite friends in and be comfortable, but they seem to want to know what's going on outside. Who's coming in? Who's getting a bus? This is their life here. They want to know; if anything happens they go right down to the drop-in room and discuss it — who said what and so and so. They call those the gossipers. they have such an empty life — they have nothing else to do, except maybe crochet or knitting. They have no interest in anything.

Actually this is not only an oversimplification, but an inaccurate evaluation by Mrs. O. of her neighbors. They may have little interest in doing anything, but they have a great deal of interest in learning about everything regarding in-house or outside events as these relate to their neighbors' lives.

Illness as a Common Bond

In any case, gossiping led many residents to keep to themselves in order to avoid the gossip mill. However, in crisis situations, and there are many at high Heaven, most of which revolve around the onset of serious illness, neighbors almost always came through with early and sustained assistance. The interesting aspect of this process is not only if someone helped, but who. Frequently help came from some unexpected quarter, i.e. persons offering the greatest help were sometimes those the person in need had previously sought to avoid. This caused the needy person to re-evaluate his opinion of his neighbors, and sometimes resulted in the emergence of fast friendships among prior enemies. In some cases the re-evaluation was more widespread, e.g. when assistance came from many sides. This led the one in need to develop a more favorable impression not only of the individuals involved, but of High Heaven in general.

Food-Centered Activities

Food and food-related activities are also very important at High Heaven. Some of these have been discussed earlier. Other food-related activities are shopping (individually or in groups), looking for food bargains, clipping coupons, exchanging recipes and discussing the day's menu with one's neighbors. These pastimes consume a good deal of one's leisure, especially, but not exclusively among the women, who outnumber the men by about 5 to 1. Food is important not only as a topic of conversation, but as a drawing card if one is trying to organize an in-house social event. In fact, the promise of food does more than anything else to overcome the residents' general apathy toward participating in planned social activities.

Other In-House Events

Other favorite pastimes at High Heaven are discussions centering around one's illnesses or those of others, playing cards and watching television. While watching television is usually a solitary pursuit, card-playing and discussing one's physical complaints are strong catalysts for much of High Heaven's social life. There are many card groups at High Heaven, most of which meet regularly in the residents' apartments, the gossip room or in the solariums. Card players generally meet at the same time and place, and with the same people; they tend to be cliquish.

The above activities account for a greater degree of interaction among residents than many of the more formal scheduled meetings, e.g. the woman's club and the men's club. There are two reasons for this. First, residents are reluctant to hold office in that one incurs with the position responsibilities and obligations that he loathes to undertake. Second, there is a general reluctance among residents to belong to formal organizations since this is seen as impinging upon their rights to do as they please, and what they are usually pleased to do is little or nothing. An example of the above was that while the women's club had few active members, and the men's club was, at the time of the study, on the verge of disbanding, Friday night bingo, another regular informal get-together, was fairly well-attended and usually drew between thirty and forty residents.

There are, of course, other activities the tenants partake of, both in and outside the facility itself. For example, while residents rarely invite each other to dinner at their apartments as this implies an obligation they would rather not incur, they do exchange food with one another, stop in to say hello, or stay for a cup of coffee. Residents also visit children and grandchildren (usually on Sunday or holidays), and their families in turn come to visit them. Finally, many residents are in regular phone contact with their children and/or other relatives who live in the area.

Most group activity at High Heaven usually takes one of the forms outlined above. The following verbatim accounts by several residents relating their day-to-day activities are illustrative.

Dr. J.:   Can you tell me about, well, I guess every day is different from the other, but what's a typical day like for you? Start with when you get up in the morning.

Mrs. S.: Well, I get up anywheres from eight to ten o'clock; it depends on how I feel. I go out and get my newspaper and then I come in and read my newspaper. I go out and get my breakfast, pick up my dishes, make my bed, run the cleaner and by that time it's pretty near noon because I'm slow. I watch the noon news (on TV), and if I'm going down the street, I go down early in the morning because there isn't such a crowd.

Dr. J.: You mean downtown?

Mrs. S.: Yes, downtown. If I'm down there in the morning, I usually stay down and have my lunch. I come home and I lay down and then I knit or crochet because I don't do much of that unless it's a bright day. (She has failing eyesight.) I go down and get my mail. That's about all of it unless it's a day when I'm going to bake or something like that. Why, then I have to spend the whole day doing that. But then on Tuesday we leave about quarter to twelve and we go up to Green Hills (a shopping center) and do our grocery shopping.

Dr. J.: How do they work that? Do you have a ride up there?

Mrs. S.: They send a bus down and we pay twenty-five cents and we go up and do our shopping and then we come back and they bring our groceries right to the elevator for us.

Dr. J.: How many generally go?

Mrs. S.: There used to be anywheres from ten to fifteen of us go over, but since the A & P store is open (only a block from High Heaven) there don't so many of us go out there because they go down to the A & P store, but we've compared prices, and Green Hills has got the freshest and the most reasonable prices of things.

Dr. J.: Where is it anyway?

Mrs. S.: Well, it's way out in the valley, it's the 1600 block I guess, and it used to be just a little roadside stand. That's what it started, but boy they've got a mammoth store there now. And then there's a shopping center out there — there's a Grants, a Fay's Drugstore, a liquor store, a ladies' furnishings store. They'll stop at all of them if you want to stop. It only costs a quarter.

Dr. J.: Then they give you time to get out?

Mrs. S.: Just about an hour, but I like to go for the ride. Well, then on Thursday, if you want to go, you can go down to the A & P store or the Victory store. The Peace Corps takes us there.

Dr. J.: So you get a free ride there, too?

Mrs. S.: Yes, we get a free ride there, and they (the Peace Corps volunteers) are awful nice. If we have to go to a doctor or to a dentist or anywhere special, all we have to do is tell him and he manages to come pick us up. Of course, we're always chicken (i.e. they rarely call on the volunteers for this purpose).*

We have a hairdresser comes here two or three times a week, I guess twice a week she comes. Well, I guess we have it pretty good here (at High Heaven) after all. I like it. I wanted to move into a different apartment. My family all voted that I stay here, they say, "Mother, you're not able to move for one thing, and it will cost you $100.00."

Dr. J.: What don't you like about this place?

Mrs. S.: I don't like some of the neighbors.

Dr. J.: You don't like some of the neighbors? You mean you'd move to another floor?

Mrs. S.: No, I'd move out of this building.

Dr. J.: Out of this building to another place?

Mrs. S.: To another place, but I'm settled here, and I've been here four years. Oh, I hate to pick up my junk because I've got more junk. . .

Dr. J.: What kinds of things, routine-like day-to-day things do you do around the building?

Mr. S.: (another resident) Well, I don't do too much around the building because I get a little tired now; I don't get up too early in the morning, and in the afternoon I'll stay here, and then I go out and take a walk around.

Dr. J.: Do you watch television much?

---

*This reluctance to use services is typical of High Heaven residents. As in the case of free legal aid noted earlier, the tenants rarely, of their own accord, avail themselves of free or inexpensive services provided by community agencies. They have to be motivated by interested outside parties such as the original coordinator in order to overcome their initial apathy.

Mr. S.: I don't during the day. After dinner I watch the television until I go to bed.* No, I think you can overdo it, especially on a colored television. That's what they tell me anyway. I don't know what the reaction is from it, but they claim it isn't too good, too much of it. Something static from it, but I don't know what it is.

Dr. J.: Do you have much to do with bingo and cards?

Mr. S.: No, I don't care too much for that.

Dr. J.: How about down in the . . . (gossip room)?

Mr. S.: I get down there and sit around with the boys. Oh, once in a while I'll go down there when they have some doings down there in the room down there, but as far as making a practice of it, it gets after a while — it gets the same routine and that's (why I don't go there much). I read a lot.

Dr. J.: You read a lot. Do you pretty much stay to yourself?

Mr. S.: I visit with the people.

Dr. J.: On this floor?

Mr. S.: On this floor, oh yes.

Dr. J.: How does that work? Do they come in for coffee and sit around and shoot the breeze?

Mr. S.: No they don't come in for coffee, but they invite me over.

Dr. J.: They invite you over and you sit around?

Mr. S.: Yeh, then I have Fred S., he's the guy next to Agnes over there. He's a veteran too; he's about fifty-six — somewhere's around there. He comes in before noon and we have a two-hour chat. He likes to chat. He don't go out much either. He used to sit down in the lobby and he would go down there occasionally. And then I go out and walk around when the weather is decent — make a day of it. . . .

Dr. J.: Can you give me an idea of what a typical day would be like if you just got up in the morning? What kinds of routines do you have?

Mrs. A.: (a third resident) I have the same old routine every day.

---

*It seems that Mr. S. considers watching TV from dinner time to bed time (about four hours a day) to be moderate by High Heaven stardards.

Dr. J.:   Well, tell me about it.

Mrs. A.: Get up and get something to eat for breakfast, then I generally make the bed, sweep the house through, go down and get my mail or if I have meals (I do that) and then maybe I come back up and watch television for a half hour or so or an hour, then go downstairs again and get the paper and read the paper — same old routine.

Dr. J.:   Do you take naps at all?

Mrs. A.: Not me, never.

Dr. J.:   Go ahead from there; you go over and eat...

Mrs. A.: Go and eat (she prepares her own meals), spend over there a couple of hours, and then I come back and maybe get a card game going and play cards for a couple of hours, come up and watch television till maybe eight, movie or something; eleven o'clock, in bed.

Mrs. R.: I was going to call you last night.

Mrs. A.: What time?

Mrs. R.: I didn't know whether that thing would be down there or not, and I didn't know if you would be out there...

Mrs. A.: Hey, I've got to get a couple of men around here to help me move my davenport. I want to clean the house. I want to get it all clean before I leave. When I come back I can't bend over to do a thing; I won't be able to bend over.

Mrs. R.: No, they said you can't with that operation.

Dr. J.:   You're having an operation?

Mrs. A.: Yeh, a...

Mrs. R.: When have you got to go?

Mrs. A.: The twenty-eighth.

Mrs. R.: Of March.

Mrs. A.: My daughter-in-law wants me to come out there, but they've got two dogs and I'm afraid, and the baby. I'm afraid it will be too much; you're not supposed to move yourself quick, and you're not supposed to bend over or to pick up everything, and I'm afraid the baby will jump on my lap, and it would be better to stay home (there in High Heaven).

Dr. J.:   The things that you do, are they usually the same people in on the card games, mostly with the same friends?

Mrs. A.: Mostly.

Dr. J.: Go over to eat with the same people and so on, and do you think the others do too?

Mrs. A.: They have their own groups. Yeh, yeh, everybody. That's what it is. We have our chapel down there too, you know, on Sunday.

Dr. J.: I know. It looked like a pretty good turn out at the mass I went to one Sunday.

Mrs. A.: There's twice as many Catholics. A lot of the Protestants go to their own church, too. They have cars or someone picks them up. My church in Liverpool, it was too far to go. Mr. Spooner used to come down and play the piano. We used to go down, wandering down ... He was very hard of hearing, and after a while he would start playing real loud, but he was a classical player. Loved to go down and listen to classical music. Oh, he was wonderful. When we had the organ in the chapel, remember? ...

Dr. J.: Do you spend a fair amount of time watching television?

Mrs. A.: I like the quiz (shows) during the daytime — the different ones.

Dr. J.: How much time every day would you say you spent watching TV? How about you Mrs. R.?

Mrs. R.: I like the stories.

Mrs. A.: I don't; those sob stories I can't (stand them).

Mrs. R.: Wednesday night, no matter if George (her husband) is downstairs shooting the breeze or if they've got a meeting or something, he usually tries to get up here to watch Adam 12, every Wednesday night. If he's a little late, it's an unusual gab session or something that they've got going on because usually ... (he is there to see Adam 12).

Mrs. A.: I like Jeopardy; I love Jeopardy (the name of a TV program).

Mrs. R.: I like spook movies.

Dr. J.: What kinds of stuff during the day ...?

Mrs. R.: Soap operas.

Dr. J.: Can you name some of the programs for me?

Mrs. R.: We watch Hollywood Matinee; after that goes off there's the Doctors with Althea, and then there's another one after that. I never pay attention to what the name of it is. I know what I want and I just ignore, tune them out until the time comes for the picture (I want to watch).

Dr. J.: How much time during a day would you say you spend watching television?

Mrs. A.: I watch them quite a bit.

Dr. J.: Two hours or so, or more?

Mrs. R.: Oh more than that, depending on how he (her husband who is ill) feels. See, when he's laying down I don't like to have it on, and sometimes he can't sleep good at night and he'll sleep late in the morning. When he's laying down sleeping, I'll crochet or knit. When he goes bowling on Wednesdays I take advantage of running the vacuum because he gets a headache, sick headache, when he hears the vacuum cleaner. If I'm not quite done when he comes back from bowling, "Aren't you done with that damn vacuuming yet?"

Mrs. A.: Ever watch Gambit, the new one? That is good.

Dr. J.: Do your friends watch TV a lot?

Mrs. A.: Yeh, everybody I know of.

Design and Architectural Problems

Other reasons motivating residents to move to alternate good inexpensive housing as it becomes available have to do with certain architectural and design features of High Heaven. For example, it was previously mentioned that High Heaven has no air conditioning, and it was further stipulated for the first three years of its existence that the tenants could not install their own. As a result the building was very hot and uncomfortable during the characteristically hot, humid summers. In fact, it was frequently five to ten degrees hotter in the apartments than it was outside, and probably fifteen degrees hotter in the enclosed hallways where residents patiently waited for the elevator.

In the last year the policy of the housing authority has changed, and the tenants are now permitted to install window air conditioners at their own expense. There are currently twelve air conditioners in High Heaven out of a total of 364 living units.

Here again, as in the case of meals available to residents in the student dining hall at reduced rates, financial considerations make the installation of an air conditioner prohibitive for most. Not only do the residents have little control over their indoor environment in summer, but they have no control over the heating in their apartments during the long winters. Apartments do not contain tenant-operated thermostats. This is not to say there is insufficient heat, but rather, whatever the temperature may be, some think it is too hot while others think it too cold. Individual preferences in the above regard and the problems it causes are particularly acute among older persons.

One way to regulate the temperature, at least if the problem is that it is too hot, is to open the window. However, this leads to another problem. High Heaven is located one-half block from an elevated major state highway, and the noise from highway traffic is so great that one cannot carry on a normal conversation within one's own apartment with the window open. (See the comments of the student in the matching program noted earlier.)

The building has other drawbacks in design. One important one is the elevators. The building came equipped with modern high-speed elevators. It soon became apparent, however, that the elderly and ailing residents were unable to reach and board the elevators before the doors closed. This left many stranded in the hot, unventilated hallway until the arrival of the next elevator. The remedy was of course to slow down the operation of the elevators. While this succeeded in providing sufficient time for residents to conveniently enter and exit the elevator, it presented a new problem of having to wait long periods of time for an elevator to become available. This problem was further compounded as the population of High Heaven changed in the direction of more chronically ill persons, an event that made waiting long periods of time for elevators difficult and sometimes hazardous. This situation might have been remedied by putting benches on each floor near the elevator so that the residents could comfortably await the elevator's arrival; however, this was contrary to the fire and building codes. The author was recently informed by a resident that this obstacle has been overcome, and that the benches were forthcoming. However, none are currently available and it is a good guess they will be a long time materializing.

Another design problem revolves around the emergency system built into each apartment for the resident's protection. This provides that the residents in an emergency may pull a cord that sticks out of the middle of the wall in the bedroom and bathroom, at which point an alarm rings and the door to his apartment automatically opens. At the sound of the alarm, a *floor representative* (there are two resident volunteer floor representatives per floor) is supposed to investigate the cause of the alarm and the nature of the crisis. The representative may in turn seek help from either of the two helpers (one, a former student) who occupy an apartment on the top floor of the building. They are on call in case of emergencies. These employees of the housing authority live rent-free and receive a small salary for their services.

This system would provide a reasonable safeguard for ailing elderly residents if not for the following: The wooden handle attached to the cord that activates the alarm sticks out of the middle of the wall. Many residents find this piece of equipment unsightly. As a result, some have either cut the pull handle off and pushed the emergency cord into the wall where it is out of sight or tied it up in a knot and hung a picture over it. In either case, the emergency system is rendered inoperative. While some alarms cannot be activated, others are activated accidentally. For example, visiting friends or relatives have sometimes mistaken the alarm cord for a light switch.

The question arises, What happens when the alarm is intentionally activated by the resident in times of real crisis? One of two things may occur: The floor representative or some other good neighbor may investigate the source of the trouble and render or seek help. On the other hand, alarms sometimes go unattended. This may happen for a number of reasons. First, residents may be afraid to leave their apartments late in the evening. Secondly, floor representatives or others may feel that they are personally unable to offer much help if any is needed, and, upon hearing the alarm, summon the paid helpers on the twenty-first floor. However, it sometimes happens that neither is available, in which case the alarm goes on ringing. Finally, there are many false alarms, and, as a result, alarms are not always taken seriously. Notwithstanding its shortcomings, the author thinks it is fair to say that the alarm system, when used appropriately, usually brings assistance. However, not all residents are confident of this. After all, residents, usually recluses, have been found dead in their apartments days after their demise and the tenants know this. In short, while residents are glad that the builders have incorporated an alarm device into their life space, discoveries such as those noted above have tempered their basic trust in the infallibility of the automatic alarm system.

Another serious architectural fault in a facility of this kind is the fact that there are no indoor connecting links between the participating units of the complex, i.e. the dorms, the student dining hall, snack bar area and High Heaven itself. This has had many untoward consequences. First is the residents' reluctance to go from one building to another (especially in the evening) because of the real and/or perceived danger. Another problem has to do with older persons negotiating their way (day or night) across the quad in cold, icy and/or slippery weather. Most residents are not that adventurous and prefer to stay within the building.

Finally, a study by a member of the faculty in the school of architecture vividly demonstrated how poorly the apartments themselves were designed for persons in wheelchairs or with other disabilities. As previously noted, many High Heaven residents suffered such disabilities.

The Plaza Floor

A final consideration, peripherally concerned with design and architectural problems insofar as they involve the use of space and facilities within High Heaven, is the county public health facility located on the *plaza floor*. While a forward-looking feature in public housing for the elderly, the public health facility has been from time to time the center of controversy and a bone of contention. Essentially, residents are divided into two camps —

those who are glad that a public health facility has been incorporated into their living space and are more or less satisfied with the services it renders, and those who are unhappy with its operation.

The latter complain that the medical examination room, incorporated into the complex in order to allow physicians, on a rotating basis, to examine the residents of High Heaven within the building itself, has never been used. Residents must still go to their own outside physicians for examinations or treatment.

Another complaint revolves about the use of the physical therapy equipment on the plaza floor. For example, the residents feel that the loom, kiln, woodworking machinery, etc., contained in the physical therapy room would make an ideal arts and crafts center. However, there is no access to the physical therapy room without the written permission of one's physician which results in this equipment and space going essentially unused. This is especially aggravating to many residents since, in their opinion, the physical therapy equipment is rarely used for physical therapy by the residents of High Heaven or the other outside clients seen by the county public health personnel.

Another bone of contention revolves around the screening practices of the public health department. As noted earlier, the plaza floor is responsible for screening potential tenants for High Heaven, and the other facilities are administered by the city housing authority. We have also seen how, in the opinion of many residents, these screening policies left much to be desired. For example, many residents were troubled by the fact that new arrivals at High Heaven are frequently not among the well-elderly, or that *undesirable elements* have been admitted more often of late. The screening process itself, i.e. the health department's evaluation of who should be placed at High Heaven or the other public housing facilities administered by the city housing authority, rested in large measure upon evaluating the potential tenant's needs and level of competence. Assuming the person seeking public housing met the age (62), residence and financial need requirements, an effort was then made to evaluate the kind of living arrangement he was best suited to. In this regard the county public health department had rented from the housing authority apartments in High Heaven which were used by potential tenants during the screening process. During their stay (the length of time varied), plaza floor personnel evaluated the tenants' ability to manage for themselves within an apartment setting. On the basis of these evaluations the public health personnel made recommendations to the potential tenant and the housing authority regarding their assessment of the best rental accommodations, giving available options. While the facilities to evaluate the potential tenants' needs and the procedures invoked to do so seemed adequate, the ultimate assessments of who went where and why seemed to many of the residents to have been ill-advised.

Finally, in order to be eligible for medical treatment on the plaza floor, one needed the consent of his physician. This rendered the prospect of in-house emergency care basically inoperative, and made ongoing support care more bother than it was worth in the opinion of some residents. The following is an example of one tenant's low opinion of the public health facility and the service it renders. Her friend, in the course of the conversation, notes some of its more positive features.

Mrs. A.: I think as far as that plaza (floor) is concerned, that it's a big fake.

Dr. J.: What do you mean?

Mrs. A.: I mean, it's definitely a fake. The nurses, you can go around the outside and look in; the light is on, and sometimes you can if the curtains are cracked. They are sitting down there and — I've gone down there so many times just to nose around and there's a lot of them (High Heaven residents) got (physical) therapy. A lot of them that could use that to much advantage, but the nurses are doing down there, they are doing nothing. I don't say they are always sitting around, but every time I've seen them ...

Dr. J.: So frequently there's a lot of facilities that nobody uses?

Mrs. A.: It's down there. What good is it?

Mrs. R.: There's a whirlpool bath, but they say you can take a whirlpool bath but you've got to get (permission from) your doctor.

Dr. J.: Permission?

Mrs. R.: Permission to take it and then it costs $10.00 to use it in the first place.

Mrs. A.: Now that's a hot one. They will take your blood pressure and your temperature if you are sick in the building.

Mrs. R.: When George (her husband) was sick I wanted them to do it and they wouldn't.

Mrs. A.: You've got to go down there.

Mrs. R.: He went down when the nurses weren't down there, when they were having their office down there — quite some time ago.

Mrs. A.: It's different now. Alice went down and Irene went down. When I came home from the hospital they came up here every day to see how I was if I stayed here.

Dr. J.: But the facilities, even when you get your doctor's okay, you have to pay for them anyway?

Mrs. R.: That's a lot of money was spent down there. What good is it? It isn't to the advantage of the people here.

Dr. J.: Do you know of any people who have ever used it?

Mrs. A.: Not anyone in here that I've ever (known).

Mrs. R.: Well, Alice goes down every day for treatment. What's her name, Alice B. — you know, the tall one . . . knitting and crocheting . . .

Dr. J.: So there's a few people, but it doesn't get to many of them.

Mrs. A.: No. I was trying to think of who she meant, but I don't. You don't mean Louise, do you — with the sugar? Is her name Louise? The one that went to the fair that time?

Mrs. R.: Yeh.

Mrs. A.: That's Louise. She has a bad case of sugar.

Dr. J.: Diabetic?

Mrs. A.: Ends up in the hospital in a coma. She goes down there, yes, but as far as her getting other than her insulin shot, I don't know if she gets anything else. Just her insulin shot as far as I know. Like I say, you talk to anybody and they say it's just a big fake. It's not doing anything, just sitting there, collecting dust.

Mrs. R.: Then too, there's supposed to be a men's, there's supposed to be a room on the other side of the plaza that's got a great big machine.

Mrs. A.: The workshop?

Mrs. R.: Yes, for the men's workshop. There's not a man in here that will go in there that can have anybody teach him to do anything. What good is it? The ones that work in here can maybe go in and use it, but there's nobody that lives here could go in there and to have somebody say, Well, I'll help you make bookends or a bookcase, anything that could be worthwhile and put in his time and say he's accomplished something.

While there is a difference of opinion among the residents regarding their experiences (and the experiences of others) with the public health facility, it is a fact that there is currently an active caseload of about 150 persons from High Heaven who are receiving service from the plaza floor in one capacity or another. Some of the ailments treated by the public health personnel were noted earlier.

THE RESIDENTS AND MENTAL HEALTH

Any consideration of public health care ought to incorporate some notion of the tenants' mental health. The residents' opinions about their environment and to some extent what they would recommend to enhance their current living arrangements have been discussed. More difficult to deal with, however, are the effects of their environment as they relate to their mental health or mental illness. The general problem of establishing objective indicators to subjective states and the abuses that have resulted from these efforts have been dealt with by Szasz, Goffman, Laing and others.* However, without undertaking a definition of mental health per se, or attempting to saw the horns off of this dilemma, some observations and impressions regarding the observable affective states of the tenants and how these can be taken as indicators of their psychological well-being are perhaps

---

*R. D. Laing, *The Divided Self*, Middlesex, Pelican Books, 1970; Erving Goffman, *Asylums*, Garden City, Doubleday, 1961; Thomas Szasz, *The Myth of Mental Illness*, New York, Dell Publishing, 1961.

in order. For example, *the presentation of self* exhibited by many of the tenants who frequent the drop-in room, the more involved gossipers notwithstanding, is characterized by *flattened affect*. They rarely interact with others; they sit by themselves and stare blankly out the window at the scene in front of High Heaven, and generally look tired, gloomy or openly depressed.

There is a second group of residents who frequent the lobby (adjacent to the drop-in room) who are generally more animated. This *heightened affect* takes on one of two forms. These will be referred to as positive and negative affects. In the former, the residents look happy and are involved in animated dialogues and other forms of positive interactions. On the other hand, the negative state of animated interaction may be characterized as *aggravated*, i.e. participants are clearly unhappy with each other, their health and/or their environment; they manifest this unhappiness by haranguing one another. These *rows* occur more often among men than women.

Another large group of persons seem to keep for the most part to themselves, but are not recluses. They see other people socially but not in the public spaces of High Heaven, e.g. the drop-in room, lobby, ladies' clubroom, men's clubroom or at bingo. Rather they visit with others from time to time in their own apartments, those of their neighbors or outside of High Heaven proper. This group of tenants, while they do not exhibit heightened affect, are fairly content with their life-styles given their age, income, past background and current state of health. They may be characterized as fairly *low key* persons who, if they are not happy, are reasonably content and rely more on informal interaction networks than formal group affiliations for socializing.

Another group (and these are dwindling in number) is the *go-getters*, organizers and *movers* of High Heaven's in-house committees, clubs and social functions. We have dealt elsewhere with their decrease in number and activity since the golden era.

Finally, there are the shut-ins. This group represents a substantial portion of High Heaven's residents. What the affective state of these social isolates is is difficult to determine.

They are rarely seen and were unavailable for interviews or observation. Other tenants, speaking of recluses in the building, feel that they were frequently depressed and generally unhappy. This is probably a fair (if unsubstantiated) intuitive appraisal.

How many residents comprise each of these groups is difficult to say. Some impressions of their relative size have been previously noted. There are, however, other indicators of the residents' states of mind. The extent and effects of alcoholism were discussed earlier. There were also a number of suicide attempts, some of which were recorded in the public health department's case records, while other suicides and attempted suicides did not receive official notice, but were recorded and conveyed by long-term residents through oral tradition.

Such impressionistic data lead one to feel that High Heaven offered fertile ground for developing counseling services and more widespread social engineering efforts as these related to improving the mental health of High Heaven residents.

STUDENT ATTITUDES TOWARD THE RESIDENTS

The residents' feelings about the extent and nature of student involvement with High Heaven have been discussed. What did the student think about the residents and their minimal involvement in the student affairs?

The university students had little or no prior knowledge or understanding of what High Heaven was designed for or the role they were to play in this unique social experiment. Three years after the first residents of High Heaven inhabited the premises, many new students arrived in the student dining hall wondering who those old people were at the table in the far corner of the room. Others, while they were aware of the twenty-one story building located across the quad, did not know who lived there or that the residents had any relationship to the student body at all.

The following excerpts from a survey of student attitudes conducted in the student dining hall and dormitory complex give some indication of their opinions of High Heaven residents.. The survey was conducted by Judy Howe, a graduate student in sociology interested in the problems of older persons. The following are edited excerpts from her notes.

Rich: Can't stand living there (in the dorms) *at all* because he hates all old people. He just doesn't like to be around them.

Karen: She feels completely neutral about the living situation. The fact that old people live there too doesn't affect her in any way. She did say, though, that while she doesn't dislike old people in any way, she feels sorry for them. She says any feelings she has toward old people are positive ones, usually it's just that she doesn't have a chance to interact with them — mainly because she doesn't go out of her way to do so.

          Karen says that some students at the dorms feel that the old people should not be allowed to eat in (the student dining hall) because they are so disgusting that they make one lose his appetite. Generally, though, most students just don't care whether or not the old people are there. She says she feels the setup (High Heaven and the experiment in intergenerational living) is a "flop," as does everyone else she knows. Some activities are planned jointly, but are not well-publicized and are poorly attended. Karen says some "matching" is attempted (matching girls who knit, etc. with residents with a similar interest), but that is not successful. Karen feels that most students feel this arrangement is artificial and not a good way to make genuine friendships.

          Karen has never seen any student-older people interaction in the dining hall with one exception. She says one resident of High Heaven is always striking up conversations with students, but that they feel he "talks their ear off," and therefore avoid him whenever possible. Generally though, there is no interaction, and the students act as if the old people are not even present.

Mike: (a visitor to the university, eating in the student dining hall for the first time.) He was amazed that such a setup existed. The mere idea was just too much for him. He tried to act like it made no difference, but he kept looking at the residents while eating. He said that when he looked at any older person, he felt he was looking at "a machine breaking down." When the older people were leaving, he stared at them intensely, laughing at their actions.

(anonymous freshman)
boy: He said that there wasn't any interaction between students and old people in the dining hall or outside of it. He had never eaten with an old person or talked to one of the residents of High Heaven. He felt that the old people segregated themselves from the students, and vice versa. He said that old people didn't seem interested in talking to the students, probably because the two groups have nothing in common. This student did not realize that the purpose of the High Heaven complex was to promote student-old people interaction. This prospect has never occurred to him, or the other students, for that matter.

Rich: (a transfer student who lives in the dorms.) Old people generally repulse him; he just can't stand to be around them. He admits that he has a real hang-up about old people, but he can't help himself. Rich said that one reason he has had a difficult time accepting old people may be because he never had any grandparents (they had all died before he was born). He finds himself unable to talk with old people. He said that an old lady tried to talk with him at a meal and that all he could think about was how to get away from her. He said that he has never attended a joint activity between the High Heaven residents and students, and neither have any of his friends. He feels that most students are indifferent about the whole thing.

Group Talk with Five Dormitory Girls

The author visited the sixth floor lounge at the dorm and talked with five students very informally. All of them agreed that there was no student-old people interaction. Several thought that if the *purpose* of the complex was better known by the students that there would be much more interaction. None were aware of the fact that the complex has been widely publicized and is nationally known....

One of the girls said that there is a male student (from the dorms) who eats in the student dining hall who cannot stand being around the old people, and that he constantly imitates them, much to the amusement of everyone. She then gave a demonstration of his imitation, much to the delight of the other students.

None of the girls had even seen an old person above the lobby of the dorm, and only a very few ever go into the lobby. They said that most students would be completely shocked if they saw an old person wandering through the halls of the dorm — students just wouldn't know what to think. Apparently students rarely go into High Heaven because a visitor's pass is required. The existence of "red tape" in High Heaven was noted by another girl who said that one reason there isn't more "interaction" is because joint programs must go through an unbelievable amount of "red tape" before they are approved. It was concluded by one girl that "red tape must be needed for security reasons."

Several of the girls in the beginning of the year did not realize that old people were supposed to eat in the student dining hall. They wondered why they were there, deciding that they had just come to watch the students out of curiosity. When the old people were still eating there some weeks later, they decided that the arrangement must be permanent.

The girls seemed to feel that the male students living in the dorms are more prejudiced toward old people than the female students. Although none of these girls had any contact whatsoever with the High Heaven residents or knew of anyone that had, one of them finally came up with the name of an R.A. in (one of the dormitories) who is in charge of planning joint dormitory-High Heaven activities. They also knew of a girl who used to visit an older woman in High Heaven frequently (adopt-a-grandparent). At that point one of the girls drew the writer's attention to a poster advertising a joint dorm-High Heaven meeting to plan for a Thanksgiving and Christmas party. The meeting was the next night at 7:00 p.m. and I attended.

Only the dorm R.A. (who was obligated to go), a friend of hers and the graduate student conducting the above survey attended the planning meeting noted above. These were the same persons previously noted who represented the students at the Thanksgiving party.

Students were not the only ones who were unaware that an experiment in intergenerational living was underway. Many of the early residents as well as more recent arrivals at High Heaven were also unaware that they were somehow involved in a social experiment in intergenerational living. It was clear that there had been insufficient groundwork laid by the housing authority and/or the university to acquaint the residents or the students with the fact that an attempt was being made to integrate students and older persons and what each might do (and why) to help such a program succeed.

The preceding discussion has described some of the features contributing to the rise and fall of a unique social experiment in intergenerational living within a campus-based retirement setting. How these life-styles compare with those in Fun City, a completely different kind of retirement setting, will be discussed in the next chapter.

FUN CITY

AN OVERVIEW

FUN CITY* is a rural, isolated tract home community of 6,000 white middle and upper class retired persons. It is situated about ninety miles southeast of a large western metropolitan area in a warm (frequently hot) valley which is relatively free from smog. The average age of the residents is seventy-one (it is listed as 63 in the *Fun City Guide*). Many residents chose Fun City over other retirement settings because it was "healthy," "peaceful," "secure," and contained other retired persons "just like us," i.e. white middle to upper class former professionals and white collar workers.

The town itself was organized around wide, well-kept streets, arranged in grid fashion and lined on both sides by wide, well-kept sidewalks. These abutted front lawns of the low-maintenance-type, i.e. gravel (sometimes dyed green) set off with one or more real or plastic bushes. Like the ranch style homes they fronted, the streets, sidewalks and other Fun City facilities were all kept immaculately clean. "Cleanliness is next to godliness" was more than an idle proverb for Fun City residents, and transgressors were soundly sanctioned.

There were three major areas of social activity in Fun City, the shopping center, the town hall-arts and crafts area and the golf club area. A fourth center, the Garden Apartments, was under construction. This facility will offer maid service and a central dining area for those residents no longer capable of tending their own homes. With its completion, Fun City will provide a full range of care for older persons, from early retirement to death.

While the Garden Apartments and town hall-activity center area were prominently displayed, the Fun City ambulance

*For a more detailed account of some of the features discussed in this chapter, see Jerry Jacobs, *Fun City: An Ethnographic Study of a Retirement Community*, New York, Holt, Rinehart & Winston, 1974.

service, rest home and mortuary, situated in that order, were inconspicuously located on the edge of town and out of sight.

Apart from these three centers of social life, Fun City gives the appearance of being deserted. Few cars travel its widen well-kept streets; fewer residents use the miles of wide, well-kept sidewalks; and even domesticated animals (and there are many in Fun City) are nowhere to be seen. They, like their masters, are home bodies or shut-ins. There is then, throughout most of the town, whether by day or night, an eerie sense of desolation.

What of those centers of social life that do promote what the developers refer to as "an active way of life"? After all, Fun City boasts ninety-two clubs and social organizations for its 6,000 residents. This would certainly seem to provide something for everyone. There is the town hall area, a staging place for large social events and lectures; the arts and crafts area; two golf clubs; two swimming pools, and a one-story shopping center housing two supermarkets, a post office, two banks and thirty-six other commercial establishments. A separate facility houses the medical center. These facilities and their use will be discussed in greater detail later in the chapter.

Apart from the social centers there are the municipal government and services. Fun City is peculiar in this regard as well; because it is an unincorporated town, it does not have its own fire department, police department, major medical facility, mayor or usual governmental apparatus.

Politically speaking, Fun City is a very conservative community, so much so that support of the United Nations is sufficient in many quarters to brand one as politically subversive. Republicans (mostly from the far right) outnumber Democrats by about 4 to 1.

Ethnically, Fun City is all white. There are no blacks and few ethnics. Data from the United States Census for 1970 notes

Total population	5,519
White population	5,516
Negro population	0
Indian population	0
Other specified races	2
Reported other races	1

In brief, Fun City is a white, middle to upper class, conservative, rural, isolated, homeowner, retirement community where an active way of life is pursued by few, and a passive way of life is pursued by many. A more detailed account of the residents' level of activity or inactivity will follow under a consideration of the comparative lifestyles of Fun City and High Heaven residents.

FUN CITY AND HIGH HEAVEN

In Chapter I a case study was presented of a novel, campus-based retirement setting, catering to ethnically-mixed, lower income persons of low educational achievement, and situated in an urban setting adjacent to a black ghetto. By all traditional sociological indicators the residents of such a retirement setting should have a very different *life chance* from those about to be described in this chapter. In fact, with regard to the usual indicators invoked within much of the literature, e.g. socioeconomic status (SES), the residents of Fun City and High Heaven should fall on the opposite end of the continuum.

The residents of Fun City are, by and large, wealthy and relatively well-educated. Those in High Heaven are poor and of low educational achievement. Fun City is situated in a warm, western, rural, isolated community, while High Heaven is located in an eastern, urban setting that spends half the year under snow and cloudy skies. Fun City residents are primarily professionals, white collar workers or skilled laborers, while High Heaven residents are recruited mainly from the ranks of unskilled labor. Fun City has no blacks and very few other ethnic minorities, while High Heaven is ethnically mixed. Fun City is a sprawling tract community of single-family dwellings, about 6,000 population, while High Heaven is a twenty-one story high-rise with approximately 420 tenants. Fun City is a very politically conservative, while High Heaven residents voted primarily Democratic, at least in local elections. Finally, Fun City, as a planned retirement setting intended to promote an active way of life, has a myriad of clubs, organizations and planned social activities while High Heaven has little to offer in this regard.

A key question arises — How different are the life-styles and value orientations of these two populations of retired persons, and to what can we attribute the difference? In what ways are they similar?

THE DIFFERENCES

Income Differential

First and foremost, income helped to contribute to a difference in life-style. In this regard, the income of High Heaven residents was much closer to the national average. In 1962 almost a third of American couples over the age of sixty-five, and almost 80 percent of nonmarried persons in that age group had incomes of $2000.00 or less. Eighty percent of High Heaven residents had incomes of $3000.00, while the average income of Fun City residents was approximately $8000.00.

The extent and effect of subsistence living on the nation's elderly was recently highlighted in an article in *Newsweek,*

> A Bureau of Labor Statistics survey revealed last fall that the basic necessities of existence — food, shelter, medical care and transportation — ate up 80.5 percent of the income of an urban retired couple living on an intermediate budget (approximately $450.00 per month) — and the squeeze has doubtless grown worse as inflation continues unchecked.
>
> An even more dismal statistic turned up in a 1973 survey by the Bureau of Research and Evaluation in Florida, home for hundreds of thousands of elderly retired persons. It found that in urban areas, 25 percent of the elderly spend less than $34.39 monthly on groceries... State researchers found that only seven percent of the urban elderly surveyed had "good dietary intake."*

Income and Housing

While High Heaven residents generally faired better than the retired elderly cited above primarily because of the good, inexpensive public housing High Heaven offered, the contrast in

---

*Down, Out — and Getting Older. *Newsweek,* October 7, 1974, p. 85.

life-styles between High Heaven and Fun City residents was much sharper. For example, most High Heaven residents lived on Social Security benefits and/or welfare payments and could not afford to purchase their own homes, while Fun City residents were almost all homeowners, many of whom paid in full for their property upon arrival. Not only could High Heaven residents not afford to purchase their own homes and retire to a preferred climate such as Fun City offered or the condominium apartments that have become increasingly popular in other retirement centers such as Florida, but they were obliged to live, in many cases, literally within four walls. This contrasted sharply with the luxurious sense of space Fun City residents enjoyed.

Apart from the living space itself or its geographical location, there was the difference in home furnishings. Most Fun City homes were furnished in what can be described as *Mediterranean modern* while High Heaven apartments made do with contemporary goodwill.

Other negative features of High Heaven living that Fun City residents did not have to contend with have been described in the preceding chapter. By reviewing these features it is obvious that Fun City residents enjoyed, at least with regard to their immediate home environment, a privileged position.

Income and Travel

Apart from being able to retire where one chose, higher income also provided for a difference in mobility patterns. For example, only about 60 of the 420 residents of High Heaven owned automobiles while nearly all of Fun City's residents owned cars, at least upon their arrival. It is true, of course, that this potential for greater mobility among Fun City residents was offset by the fact that High Heaven was situated in the center of an urban area and serviced by municipal transportation while Fun City had, at the time of the study, no intracity transportation and next-to-no intercity connecting links. As a result, Fun City residents had to have automobiles in order not to be completely isolated. One irate citizen voiced her discontents in an article in the *Fun City News*. Such public outcries were unusual in that residents were very reticent to openly lodge complaints. There was a tacit understanding among Fun City residents that one neither easily gave nor took offence, and certainly not in the public domain. Excerpts from the article are given below.

> I walk through the streets and there is no sign of life. I see women with heavy bundles trudging up the road from the shopping center and wonder how much longer they can take it.
>
> The Civic Association discusses everything but transportation... If money can be spend on repairs for the lawn bowling, shuffleboard courts and closed-circuit television, some should be spend on humanity. I understand there are fifteen hundred persons without transportation in Fun City. The people without transportation have two alternatives — move into an apartment that costs more, or into the new Fun City Garden Apartments where prices are more than most people can pay. (These two facilities are located near the shopping center and town hall activity center).
>
> Transportation was guaranteed when people signed the papers (to move into Fun City). It was in the literature also. The people were told not to worry. "It would be taken care of." People bought on that premise.

As a result of this lack of public transportation, many Fun City residents were socially isolated. The reasons why so many automobile owners did not drive or restricted their driving will be discussed later in the chapter when the question of similarities is considered.

A further consideration regarding differences in resident travel is its nature, extent and duration. Some Fun City residents regularly took European trips and round-the-world cruises. In fact, many jet setters considered Fun City as much as a home base for foreign and domestic travel as they did a home. There were also the trailer, camper and boating sets. A large compound on the outskirts of town was specifically designated for the storage of travel and recreational vehicles belonging to Fun City residents. This leisure travel and sport activity was not a part of High Heaven living. When one traveled it was to see children, grandchildren or other relatives, or perhaps to go to Florida for a week or two during the winter. Travel styles, then, as part of the life-style were also economically influenced.

Natural vs. Unnatural Settings

Another key difference between Fun City and High Heaven was the way in which new arrivals encountered their environment during the early stages of settling in. In both cases this took some getting used to, but there was a different sense in which this feeling was experienced. Some residents of High Heaven came from a background of poor housing, and for them High Heaven offered almost luxurious accommodations that required some getting used to. Other residents had previously been homeowners and moved from three or four-bedroom homes into one-room apartments in High Heaven. This, too, required some getting used to, but these differences required an accommodation to one's environment that was qualitatively different from that experienced by Fun City residents. The major difference revolved around the notion of natural vs. unnatural environments.

The key fact in this regard was that Fun City had no children, young adults or ethnic minorities. It is true of course that many older persons· are glad to be free of the confusion that children bring and the constant attention that they require. For example, while many Fun City residents were happy to see their children and grandchildren (they saw precious little of them), they were also glad to see them leave so that they could return to the low stress environment they sought and that Fun City so ably provided. Residents of High Heaven were also bothered by children from the adjacent black ghetto who used the campus area next to High Heaven to ride their bicycles, yell at the tenants and, generally, from the residents' point of view, make a nuisance of themselves. While part of the residents' indignation stemmed from the fact that the children used their facilities in this way, less of their discontent stemmed from the fact that they were children than the fact that they were black.

In any case, while some residents enjoyed seeing students and children near or about High Heaven and others resented it, neither considered it in any way unnatural. On the other hand, the complete lack of children and/or young adults in Fun City led many new residents to consider their environment unnatural even if they were glad or at least ambivalent about this state of affairs.

After all, if one had lived for seventy years in the outside world, one saw or at least knew of all kinds of people. It is no idle proverb that "it takes all kinds to make a world." Insofar as one did not encounter, for the first time in his life, all kinds, Fun City was experienced by many residents as unnatural and a place that took some getting used to. In short, new residents in Fun City experienced a form of culture shock.

There were other unnatural things about Fun City. It was noted earlier how peculiar it was to enter a fully inhabited town of 6,000 persons that gave the appearance of being uninhabited. Quiet, peaceful or sleepy town maybe, but dead town in a sense that it is invoked here immediately implies a sense of peculiararity. The lack of activity and the other usual signs of life such as litter, moving autos or persons, animal excrement or background noises is eerie. It is true of course that residents chose to come to Fun City for the peace and quiet, law and order and company of their own choosing, but all of these, confronted for the first time in the configuration they formed in Fun City, proved too much of a good thing for many new arrivals. Such a gestalt was encountered as Martians would encounter the earth — as an alien environment.

The following are illustrative excerpts taken from the tape-recorded interviews.

Mr. B.:   In general, I think I said before, most of the people (in Fun City) are happy that they retired here.

Mrs. B.:   I don't think so. It is very unnatural if you want my opinion. Personally I think it's unnatural. Because youth needs age and age needs youth. We have to have all kinds in order to have a normal community.

Mr. W.:   We lived in Beverly Hills for forty-two years.

Mrs. W.:   And it takes a lot of adjustment (to get used to Fun City). It takes quite a little bit of time. We're not real thrilled about everything all of a sudden, you know. It takes a bit of adjustment to leave your friends and come to *some place entirely different.*

It's entirely up to you whether you're happy or not (in Fun City). You can sit home and be very unhappy or you can enter into things and be very happy. It's entirely

up to the individual. Nobody's gonna come knocking
on your door and invite you to go any place. You have to
go...

Mr. W.: Otherwise they completely ignore you.

Mrs. W.: There's been a lot of unhappy people (here) and a lot of
them have moved away (because) they've been unhappy.

A third woman: It doesn't really disturb me, but I just don't know
how to say it. You see nothing but old faces (in the Fun
City shopping center). Do you know what I mean? It
seems that it's a little nicer to go shopping and see
everything, you know, children and all ages. I don't
want to have it (children and the noise) right next door,
but still I like to get out into where I have a little
more... Maybe I shouldn't feel that way. I'm old, too.
I'm not young any more, but still I think it's kind of odd
to see (only old faces in Fun City).

Planned Social Activities

Another stark difference between Fun City and High Heaven is
the extent of planned social events. Fun City offers its residents
ninety-two clubs and organizations for their enjoyment. The *Fun
City News* (the community newspaper) lists about 150 planned
social events every week; about sixty-five morning activities, sixty
afternoon and twenty-five evening events. Some indication of the
extent and nature of these activities as taken from the *Fun City
Guide* is given, "Golf association (men's): 312 members; golf
association (women's): 104; golf association (women's) The
Niners: 53 members; golf association (men's) North Course: 107;
and golf association (women's) North Course: 168 members."

Card clubs also have large paper memberships. For example,
bridge club (party contract): 650 members; bridge club
(duplicate): 110; canasta club: 100; and pinochle club: 125
members.

The arts and crafts club lists a total of 198 members. These are
divided between the woodshop and ceramic, art, lapidary and
sewing classes. Also included in the same complex but as part of a
separate unit is the camera club with 141 members.

Add to this the square dance club of 250 members, the bicycle club of 139 members, the shuffleboard club of 130 members and lawn bowling with 142 members, not to mention the memberships in the smaller hobby clubs, e.g. stamp club, chess club, checkers club, etc., and it would seem that there is, among Fun City residents, an active participation in social clubs and sports of every kind.

The planned social events at High Heaven pale by comparison. These were discussed in some detail in the preceding chapter. However, here, as in the case of travel, transportation and politics, these differences are more apparent than real. This aspect will also be considered in some detail later in the chapter under the discussion of similarities in life-styles.

Medical Services

Another major difference between Fun City and High Heaven is the availability and accessability of major medical services. In this regard the residents of High Heaven were at a distinct advantage. High Heaven was literally surrounded by private hospitals. In addition, a Veterans Administration medical faciilty was a block away, and a major university research and medical center complex was within walking distance.

In contrast, Fun City had (at the time of this study) no inpatient medical facilities for its 6,000 elderly and ailing residents. There was only an outpatient medical center staffed by four overworked doctors who, because of their caseload, refused to see new patients. In short, many residents had, within the city limits, access to no medical services at all.

> Well, the medical problem is another problem we have. I guess you probably know something about it...We don't have enough doctors to put it bluntly, in the first place. We don't have enough doctors because we don't have a hospital yet. Doctors don't like to come where there isn't a hospital you know. They want facilities and X-ray and all the lab facilities and we don't have those ... The doctors just don't take any more patients. They can't, they are overworked...
> If I went in right now and called to one of these doctors (in

Fun City) and said I'd like to get to the doctors, they would say
"We are sorry but we can't take you." You'll have to go to the
emergency (room) in Missionville (about 15 miles away).

Those who were being seen at the medical center on an
outpatient basis had no access to major inpatient medical
services, and had to drive or be driven fifteen to thirty miles (one
way) to the nearest hospital in the event of a crisis or for routine
appointments. Many, indeed most, of Fun City's residents, were
obliged to acquire major medical services in this way. This
problem was further compounded by Fun City's geographic
isolation and the almost complete lack of public intercity
transportation.

Security

How did Fun City and High Heaven compare with respect to
security? In the preceding chapter the lack of security High
Heaven had to contend with and its ubiquitous effects upon the
tenants' social life were dealt with. How did the residents of Fun
City fare on the question of security? For a population of white
middle to upper class homeowners who specifically chose Fun
City for retirement because it offered, above all else, security, they
fared not as well as they had hoped.

Among the many peculiar features of Fun City was the fact that,
as an unincorporated town, it had no police department or fire
department; it had to rely upon the state highway patrol and
county fire department for service. There was, of course, Fun
City's natural advantage with respect to security, i.e. its
geographic isolation. Very few outsiders stopped or shopped in
Fun City. While its isolation kept it from coming to the attention
of society's more unscrupulous elements (apart from some of the
Fun City realtors and shopkeepers themselves), it offered little
protection from crimes against property or person should a
resident be selected as a target for criminal activities. The
following is some indication of its vulnerability. An item in the
Fun City News notes,

> Fun city is the safest community as far as crime is concerned
> among all of the cities under the jurisdiction of the sheriff's

substation, the captain told the (Fun City) *News* this week. This despite the fact that there has been a recent rash of burglary crime and an attempted mugging here. The captain said his office has taken all the necessary steps for patrol protection of Fun City, plus other measures to curb such offences.

Perhaps a more unobtrusive measure of the residents' feelings of insecurity, notwithstanding the safe-in-the-streets contentions of the Chamber of Commerce or those mouthed by the residents, is the fact that scarcely anyone walked in the streets. This was true not only during the frequently hot daylight hours, but in the cool of evening as well. The question arises, Why did the residents not take strolls more often? All of Fun City's wide, well-kept streets were lined on both sides with wide, equally well-kept sidewalks. The answer, given or implied during the taped interviews, was, it's safe in Fun City — but not that safe. In fact, residents always kept their screen doors and front doors locked, always left lights burning, had neighbors keep an eye peeled for suspicious characters when they were away for a day or so, and frequently harbored little barking dogs.

In short, while Fun City residents came to Fun City in order to escape the crime-in-the-streets they associated with big city living, they did not in fact feel secure, at least not that secure in Fun City.

Shopping Facilities

Shopping facilities, apart from fulfilling the obvious need of conveniently offering goods and services, meet the equally important need of providing a staging area for social interaction. In this regard one Fun City resident had this to say, "There are a lot of people that buy their supplies daily too. A lot of my friends go to the store everyday and buy what they are going to eat that day. I think it is part of their social life... They like to go down and meet all their friends. I think that's a lot of what fills the stores up; it's those everyday shoppers." Shopping, as a social event, was true of High Heaven residents as well. This has already been discussed in the preceding chapter.

How did Fun City and High Heaven compare with regard to convenient and plentiful shopping? Because of its geographical isolation and the lack of intercity transportation, the Fun City shopping center was an essential part of Fun City living. This by no means meant that residents were content with the prices, services or the availability of the shopping center — many were not. There was, at the start of the study, only one supermarket in Fun City, and in the the opinion of many residents, it abused its monopolistic standing. Prices were considerably higher than in the markets in adjacent towns, and service was neither quick not courteous. Since then, a second supermarket has opened, and, while prices are not yet competitive, they are lower than before, and service has improved.

Mrs. E.: When it isn't convenient to get out (to do out-of-town shopping) you can get most everything down there (at the Fun City shopping center) but shoes and clothes...

Mr. E.: Now with Safeway in there competing with Mayfair (the two competing supermarkets noted above) it's been much better.

Mrs. E.: And we have a new drug store. They had a monopoly and they overcharged. And now there are two drugstores, and as soon as we get two of everything it will help...

Mr. E.: So you see they could practically set their own prices here and they did. So most of us, well we shop at the commissary over at (the nearby military base.). I'm a retired officer so we shop there and a lot of the officers do so we don't shop here much at all.

Apart from the supermarkets, there were three eateries in Fun City — two coffee shops located in the shopping center and one across the street at the Fun City Motel and Restaurant. While prices were competitive at the eateries, prices in the other service and commodity shops were overpriced, and choices were limited. Because of this, many residents would drive once or twice a week to a nearby town. Retired military personnel, and there were many in Fun City, went to the post exchange to do a week's shopping at one time. This served two purposes — it saved money and offered a day's outing for the residents. Some further indication of the residents' discontents with the Fun City shopping center is evident in the following verbatim account from one of the transcribed taped interviews.

> The shopping is very disheartening here. That's one of the most frustrating things. And I think that's why Mission (another nearby retirement setting) grew with such leaps and bounds as they did because women like it because it was near the shopping centers. (Women in Fun City outnumber the men by 3 to 1. In High Heaven it was 5 to 1.) You see it gave them a place to go shopping, and that always makes for a lot of contentment, believe me, to be able to get to the stores (and) see things... That's one of the women's biggest gripes.

Apart from price and selection, there was the question of availability. The Fun City shopping center (as well as the planned social activities) were not easily available to all Fun City residents. The primary reason for this was the lack of public transportation.

> Well, public transportation (within or out of Fun City) is bad, Mr. Jacobs. (There was) a little bus that ran around town once an hour, and it was a very good little thing for people who didn't have cars... But when (the developer) quit this thing (about 6 months prior to the study), we now have nothing. And that's one of the cries of the community for those people who don't drive. There's no way to get downtown (to the shopping and activity centers).

While this makes local shopping difficult for some, it makes competitive shopping at nearby towns or the post exchange impossible for many. There was essentially no way out of Fun City by public transportation. There were two exceptions. One is a private cab service and car rental that is very expensive and excludes the possibility of its routine use. For example, this service charges twenty-five dollars to drive a resident to the airport twenty-five miles away where for twenty dollars he can fly to a major city and tourist attraction 500 miles away. A second possibility is the Greyhound Bus Service that was recently initiated in Fun City on a trial basis. This offered a once-a-day trip to a nearby town where residents might, with some effort, go shopping and return the same day. It is fair to say that while there were differences in needs and opinions, most residents felt shopping in Fun City left much to be desired.

If Fun City shopping was cause for resident discontent, how did it compare with that in and around High Heaven? There was only one small market that was actually a part of the High Heaven complex. The residents felt that the merchandise there was overpriced and the selection, poor. As a result, those who were physically able to go elsewhere did so. This was not difficult since there were many options. For example, for twenty-five cents a private bus stopped at High Heaven and picked up shoppers, delivered them to a shopping center and returned them to High Heaven when they were through. More recently a large supermarket opened only two blocks away from High Heaven, and the shops and department stores that are a part of most downtown areas were (for most residents) within walking distance. The others could easily catch city buses (which stopped in front of High Heaven) to and from the downtown area for a nominal senior citizens' fare. Certainly High Heaven shoppers had a greater latitude of conveniently-located shopping than was the case in Fun City. However, there were mitigating circumstances that led the residents of High Heaven and Fun City to feel they were unfairly isolated from good shopping. These revolved around problems of security and transportation respectively, and will be dealt with in greater detail later in the chapter.

Church and Church Functions

What role did the church play in the life-styles of Fun City and High Heaven residents? As mentioned in Chapter I, High Heaven had a chapel that was shared primarily by Protestants and Catholics. There had, on a couple of occasions been a rabbi to preside over Jewish services on holidays, but there were so few Jews living at High Heaven that it was decided to discontinue Jewish services since it was unlikely there would be a minion (the 10 adult Jewish males required for the services to begin).

For the most part, the chapel facilities were shared by Catholics and Protestants. Sunday services were usually well-attended, indeed better attended than most other High Heaven functions.

Going to chapel on Sundays or holidays was, for many, an important event on their weekly round of activities. However, not all High Heaven residents used the chapel. Many continued to frequent the churches they had attended in different parts of the city before moving to High Heaven, and in that way managed to keep in touch with old friends in their former neighborhoods.

Another feature of religious life as it related to the residents' social lives was church lunches. These were sponsored by several community churches and offered good inexpensive lunches at conveniently-located downtown centers. About twenty High Heaven residents (almost all women) routinely attended these functions which provided not only a nutritious and inexpensive lunch, but another way of spending a couple of hours outside of High Heaven in the company of old community-based friends.

In summary, there was a fairly active sector of High Heaven residents who were regular church-goers, and who either attended the High Heaven chapel, outside services in the greater community, and/or church functions such as the lunch or volunteer programs. Other residents, however, did not attend chapel services because they preferred keeping to themselves. In this manner they avoided giving or taking offence, something that might always occur if one did not carefully choose one's company. This aspect was discussed in the preceding chapter with respect to Fun City's interaction patterns. Here, as in other High Heaven social settings, not attending chapel services helped keep them out of the gossip mill.

How did Fun City's church and church-related activities compare with High Heaven's? In churches, as in social clubs, Fun City had something for everyone. There were eight churches listed in the *Fun City Guide* (a pamphlet listing all of the clubs, churches and activities in Fun City). Churches and their memberships were entered in the *Guide* as follows, "Catholic church: 700 members; Lutheran church: 200 Methodist church: 1450; Progressive Reform Judaism: 70; Temple Beth Shalom: 125; United Church of Fun City: 550; Seventh Day Adventists: 20; and the Church of Jesus Christ of the Latter Day Saints: 60 members." This list does not include church-related social groups who do volunteer work and arrange church socials for their members and the community at large. Once again the question arises, How active was this paper membership? One would expect a white middle class tract home retirement community to have an above-average active membership. However, many Fun City church-goers felt that attendance at religious services were less than gratifying. In fact, one estimate made by a retired army chaplain currently active in church affairs puts active memberships at about the national average.

> But of course you realize in a community like this, just like any other, your church people, including all different groups, run about 25 percent. But there are a lot of people that are in benevolent causes that support service clubs and masonic groups that are not particularly interested in church, that is, are not members.

If the number of Fun City residents attending religious services was in no way exceptional, the number of more active residents engaged in church socials and/or volunteer-related work was. A great many residents engaged in a variety of volunteer projects. However, while some of these served to promote forms of social interaction among the participants, others were solitary pursuits. For example, many volunteer projects were of the take home variety. Some of these activities are outlined below.

> We don't just come here to sit and play cards, all of us... There are a lot of very worthwhile things that are done by the people (of Fun City) by service organizations, by women's clubs, news clubs, church groups, all the organizations.
>
> Let me start with our own church. I belong to the United Church here as a kind of working member. First of all, we have a project around Jonesville area (a black rural ghetto adjacent to Fun City). This is a pocket of poverty there, people who have come out from the metropolis, blacks, Mexicans and whites, all living together quite harmoniously, but many of 'em in need. And when I came down here (to Fun City) I saw that need and started in to get our church interested in it and we have done a great deal over the last five years.
>
> We have made direct help with families working through the welfare department. They tell us when a family is in desperate need and we help out.
>
> Maybe a family makes an application for instance, and they

have to wait for their applications (to be processed). They have no food, clothes, place to live, nothing. The welfare lets us know and we try to do something about it... The *clothes closet* and *food cupboard* (the church gives food and volunteered clothing to the needy). The first six months (of last year) we serviced 200 families (outside of Fun City) in this valley. We also make baby layettes for needy children. One year we made several hundred. My wife happened to be in charge of that particular phase of it... We also made school bags, you know, with crayolas, pencils, tablets, erasers and pencil sharpeners. We made nearly 200 of those.

If church groups helped the less fortunate residents of Jonesville, it was from afar. They did not actually go to Jonesville proper or participate in their affairs.

Mrs. R.: I was coming to that (the conspicuous absence of blacks in Fun City). We have Jonesville. Jonesville as far as I know hasn't really changed in thirty or thirty-five years. I don't even think they have painted anything (homes and businesses). It's a poor community. They (the residents of Fun City) resent this community. For example, on Thanksgiving Day they had a celebration, the Chamber of Commerce (of Jonesville) did. I and (a relative of hers) went. We were the only two people there from Fun City. It's only ten minutes away, you know.

Worthy of separate note is the Jewish congregation. While there were only about 150 Jews in Fun City out of a total population of 6,000, they represented by far Fun City's more politically liberal element. Their friends (whether Jews or gentiles) were also usually recruited from the towns more liberal elements.

The Jewish synagogue was converted Baptist church, and the Jews, probably more than any other Fun City religious group, attended the Church of their choice more from social than religious needs. Many Jews, while immersed in their cultural heritage, were closer (religiously speaking) to practicing agnostics or atheists than practicing Jews and openly said so.

Mr. W.: I belong to the temple. We are not religious people. I told them (the congregation) that. In fact I'm a downright atheist. But there is a small Jewish group here which we

are members of. I went there (to the temple); they were
paying honor to someone (who had died) and I didn't
know the man, but... I was very much impressed with
the warmth, the fellowship, (and) they were so happy for
us to come there. I said after going there, "You know," I
said, "I think we should belong to the temple." And I
told them, I said not for any religious purpose, but
purely social.

The reason why the temple was so important in serving as a
social center had to do, at least in part, with the fact that Jews were
not overly popular with other Fun City residents. This was true
because many of the retired Jews in Fun City had Jewish accents
and other mannerisms that made it abundantly clear that they had
not melted into the melting pot. In short, the Jews stood out in a
social environment that was designed above all else to level
differences. Secondly, because the Jews were politically more
liberal than most Fun City residents, this too worked to set them
apart. Some indication of these political and cultural differences
and how they worked against their being able to establish
meaningful social relationships is given below.

Mr. B.: I'm trying to organize a chapter (of the United Nations
Association in Fun City). Well, a lot of people that I
approach and speak to say this is a Communist
organization, and that settles it.

Dr. J.: How does that affect your friendships with your
neighbors?

Mr. B.: Well... we like to be neighborly and friendly and if I
speak to someone and if his views don't coincide with
mine, well, right away we'll change the subject. We'll talk
about fishing.

Dr. J.: Change the subject?

Mr. B.: We'll talk about fishing or hunting or something like
that, do you see? That's the best way. And lately, you
know, this business with the bombing, Nixon's bombing
the North Vietnamese. He (the neighbor) is 100 percent in
favor of it. *Now how can you be friendly when your
political views are so different?* (Emphasis added)

One not only censors one's unpopular political views, one

censors everything lest it get into the gossip mill. This was especially true for Jews.

Mr. B.: Sometimes we get together in their house (their neighbor's) or mine and play a game of cards and spend a few hours and then have a cup of tea and talk. *And we try to avoid gossip. That's the most important thing, see....* Before I've finished a sentence (that he has spoken to his wife) the rest of the town knows it, so you have to be on the lookout. *And especially amongst the Jews, it's a very small town.* (Emphasis added)

It is not surprising to find that while Jews might belong to social clubs, they were not joiners. Furthermore, the clubs they were involved in were not those in the Fun City limelight. For example, the Jews contributed mightily to Fun City's small chess club.

Contact with Relatives

How did the retired persons in Fun City compare with those in High Heaven regarding the nature and extent of contact with their relatives? For the most part the residents of High Heaven faired much better. Many had children and grandchildren who lived in town. It was noted in the previous chapter that most residents of High Heaven were either natives of the area or long-term residents as were their brother, sisters and childhood friends. As a result, High Heaven residents were visited by children, and grandchildren and other relatives or vice versa more often than Fun City residents. In addition to visits, many were in daily phone contact. This contrasted sharply with Fun City where one rarely ever saw visitors. Visits here were infrequent and were frequently a mixed blessing. For example, some visitors were more motivated by a desire to borrow money or receive other assistance from well-to-do parents rather than to see or be with them. Such instances generated much resentment on the part of parents.

Visits from grandchildren also disrupted the residents' peace and quiet. Children made noise, were disorderly and occasionally broke things or otherwise shattered the perfect tranquility characteristic of Fun City living.

While it was true that many residents viewed visits as a mixed blessing, residents, even when ambivalent about visitors, were hurt by how few visits they received.

By contrast, High Heaven residents seemed to be less sensitive to the disruptive effects of visiting relatives and saw more of their children and grandchildren than Fun City residents. In fact, in High Heaven, when residents traveled it was usually to visit distant relatives. This, too, was much less the case in Fun City where travel was more often associated with vacationing.

Part of this difference in the extent of contact with relatives may be attributable to the fact that not only did High Heaven residents have more relatives, but they were more accessible. High Heaven relatives lived nearby, frequently in the same city, while the relatives of most Fun City residents lived ninety miles away in the metropolis or its suburbs.

However, there were other mitigating factors as well. It was not only that there were more High Heaven relatives with easier access, but the nature of family interaction patterns among the lower class residents of High Heaven differed appreciably from those in Fun City. There was a closeness that is characteristic of primary relationships that was lacking in Fun City's families. This is not to say that all residents of High Heaven got along well with their children or grandchildren — they did not, but they had more children, and from this greater number came greater choice. They got along well with some and not with others. Fun City residents had smaller families. If one did not get along with an only child, one had little or no contact with his child or grandchildren.

In short, because of accessability the nature of interactions and the pool of relatives available to choose from, High Heaven residents were in closer and more frequent contact with relatives than Fun City residents. This worked for many as might be expected — to lessen feelings of loneliness and isolation among High Heaven residents, notwithstanding the loneliness and sense of isolation that so many of the residents in both settings felt.

The Similarities

Some of the ways in which the lifestyles of Fun City and High

Heaven residents differed have been considered. Let us not consider some of the ways in which they were the same. Many of the same aspects discussed under differences will be considered, but not necessarily in the same order.

Income

For those who have experienced poverty and those who have not, there is the easily recognized fact that if "man does not live by bread alone," it helps. Having sufficient income to insure that one can retire where he wants, in the kind of setting he prefers, and among those of his own choosing is seen as a very definite asset in the ledger of later life. Indeed, if there is any chance for happiness and contentment during this period of the life cycle, it is seen to lie in having sufficient funds to enjoy the leisure ones long-awaited retirement promised. We have already indicated that the residents of Fun City had these funds and those of High Heaven did not. The question is, Did money buy happiness? The answer is, it seems not.

Many independently wealthy persons in Fun City spent a great deal of time enveloped in anticipatory anxiety regarding their future economic security or that of their spouse. In addition to this sense of insecurity (economic and otherwise) that went undiminished by the extent of their real assets, there was the fact that Fun City residents were generally unhappy in the retirement setting of their choice. This was true of many High Heaven residents as well. For example, the latter would have preferred a warmer climate, not living adjacent to the black ghetto, greater personal and economic security, and *living among their own kind*, i.e. in an *all white* setting. In short, High Heaven residents would have wanted (given the choice) everything Fun City residents had. The irony is, or course, that so many of Fun City's residents, who were able to afford and felt they had bought into all of this, were just as unhappy as the High Heaven residents who could not.

Why was this true? One would intuitively have expected that if these two retirement settings were polar opposites, as it seems they are, then if one group was relatively unhappy, the other should have been relatively happy, but by and large, this was not true. The reason for this probably was that while there were many obvious differences between these two retirement settings, they were outweighed by the more subtle but profound similarities.

That status and economic security does not necessarily lead to happiness or contentment is in no way a new notion. Durkheim and others noted that the suicide rate was highest among the upper classes, and that it increased directly with age. With this in mind, what was it that led to the widespread unhappiness experienced by Fun City and High Heaven residents, SES notwithstanding?

Isolation

Perhaps the major contributing factor to this unhappiness was the feelings of isolation and the lack of or diminishing base for meaningful social relationships. Indeed, in a formal sense it is these same feelings that lead persons of all ages and walks of life to experience "the end of hope" and "suicidal ideation."* Under these circumstances it is not surprising that the rate of suicide increases with age. How Fun City and High Heaven residents were subject to, and inadvertantly self-imposed constraints that led to a state of diminishing reciprocal meaningful interactions with others has been shown. This occurred on many fronts. Reference to suicide and alcoholism in High Heaven was noted in the preceding chapter; the same was true in Fun City.

Mrs. R.: It somehow or other got around that I had been a counselor. I got two phone calls during the last year that I would say created in me fears of imminent suicides. I referred them to the local crisis center (in a neighboring town), and suggested that they go over and perhaps speak to the people at the mental health center.

Dr. J.:   There were a couple of residents who called?

Mrs. R.: Yes, that knew me casually and wanted me to come over,

---

*See Jerry Jacobs, *Adolescent Suicide*, New York, John Wiley & Sons, 1971; A. L. Kobler and E. Stotland, *The End of Hope*, New York, Free Press of Glencoe, 1964.

you see, "come right over, I'm so frightened," there were other clues you know...You can find yourself in a quagmire of melancholia, maladjustment and severe neurosis here (in Fun City). I think there have been a number of accidents. I think many of them aren't accidents.

The Fun City liquor store located in the shopping center was also one of Fun City's most flourishing small business establishments. The author, during the course of the home interviews, was frequently offered drinks, and a few of Fun City's more outspoken residents volunteered that there was, in fact, a lot of heavy drinking in Fun City. Finally, the bar at the Queens Inn (Fun City's only restaurant, motel and cocktail lounge) did a brisk business, especially by Fun City standards. While drinking was a subrosa activity both in High Heaven and Fun City, it was better concealed by Fun City residents.

What were some of the factors that contributed to these feelings of unhappiness and despair? First were the outside constraints imposed upon them by their social and natural environments. These frequently did not manifest themselves until after the move to the retirement setting had been accomplished. For example, residents moving to Fun City were, upon arrival, usually in fair health and able to drive. Nearly all had automobiles. As a result, the lack of intracity or intercity public transportation initially presented no serious problem. Then, too, there was the planners' promise that public transportation was just around the corner. However, several years later (many of the residents interviewed were long-term residents) things looked very different. Their health had deteriorated badly; many had poor eyesight, heart ailments or poor reflexes, and could no longer drive, or, if they could, their mobility was limited to driving during daylight hours and/or only around town and off the freeways. Many drove against medical advice or without a valid drivers licenses. This was not surprising when one realizes that not driving means that one is, for all intents and purposes, socially isolated. The promised public transportation never materialized. Depending upon where in Fun City one was situated, not driving meant losing access to the shopping center, activities center and limited medical facilities. It also meant the loss of access to outside medical aid, travel or shopping breaks. It meant in fact that nondrivers were effectively isolated from everyone but their immediate neighbors. This would in some cases suffice to sustain some critical and necessary links with others. The following is an example taken from the taped interviews.

> I have neighbors on both sides of me that just drive me mad. I don't think this woman has ever had visitors or visited. I'm the only person who ever goes there. They've never been down to town hall. She's going almost totally blind now. She's been a diabetic, but she's been that all her life. And now you see this one (other neighbor) over there is a fairly young woman, a beautiful woman in her early fifties, but she's almost a mental case because she babies herself so and imagines that she's sick . . . I've got 'em all around me. The one across the street is just as bad. But they expect me to come to them all the time and, of course, like a nut, I do. And I run around and go to see them all.

However, many Fun City residents did not count their neighbors among their friends. Many had only one or two close friends (often long-standing friendships that preceded their arrival in Fun City) who lived across town. Not being able to drive to visit friends or have them visit effectively isolated many Fun City residents from establishing or maintaining forms of meaningful social relationships. The ecology of the town, its geographic isolation from other cities, the lack of intracity and intercity public transportation and the rapid and unexpected deterioration of the residents' health all contributed to bring this about.

These were some of the structural and natural factors contributing to the residents social isolation. Other limiting factors upon the nature and extent of interaction were self-imposed. This hinged upon the key tacit understanding of the residents that they not easily give or take offence in the name of keeping the peace. This resulted, as was noted earlier in the chapter, not only in decreased interaction, but in decreased meaningful interaction. Fun City residents tended to avoid controversial topics and, like High Heaven residents, also sought to avoid the gossip mill. This strategy led to trivial forms of interaction and/or total disengagement.

The author does not mean to imply that *all* Fun City residents were affected in the same way by these factors — they were not. As previously noted, about 500 of Fun City's 6,000 retired citizens were actively engaged in one or more of the many clubs and social organizations Fun City had to offer. Such involvement, apart from providing a means of coping with leisure, also offered continual and plentiful settings for establishing ongoing and meaningful forms of interactions with others. Those among the active minority reaped the benefits of plenty to do. In fact, others who were not a part of the formal planned social activities also managed to establish and maintain interactions with others. These included persons previously discussed who had only one or two close friends in the community, saw a lot of them, and had little to do with Fun City planned social life. Many of these were also relatively content with Fun City living.

However, it was the Fun City shut-ins or social isolates who were not actively involved, or contentedly disengaged, with the exception of a few close friends, who were most unhappy. Unfortunately, these represented the largest segment of the population.

Apart from those who enjoyed Fun City or those who could take it or leave it, there were those who were socially isolated and openly hostile.

Mrs. O.: The representative member of this community is a neurotic, maladjusted person. This goes regardless of how they might describe themselves because this is not a normal community. It's plastic and a place where everyone already has his hole already picked out — they just haven't had sense to lie down in it yet. I'm including the golfers (and) the bridge players. It is also a community in which I've seen selfishness developed to an unparalleled degree. Such a degree of egocentricism I would say borders on the pathologic. If we put neuroses, let's say on a continuum, we're all neurotic. We live in a sick society so we're all sick a little bit, but let's say these would all be way over on the plus side. There is a drinking problem here. It is extremely well hidden, but there. Have you interviewed any of the local physicians?

Dr. J.:   No, not yet.

Mrs. O.: I have. They estimate that over 80 percent of their clientele have no organic defects of no functional (disorders)... In many cases they (the Fun City residents) were willing to pay for the visit, just for the fifteen minutes, to talk to someone. Now all of this, it's like, let's say you look at a beautiful clear pond, but the water is not potable, and you would never discover this until you took a dip... There is no altruism here, I haven't seen it. There is no, there is very little humanity. You have a bunch of aging hoaks who are concerned only with prolonging the period during which they can walk around without actually lying down (on the ground). Well, it's not from any point of view a normal community. You (find) very little willingness amongst people to cooperate with each other. Each one is boxed up in his own little box and (it) has all eight sides of the cubes carefully locked, sealed and bolted. The entire community it would seem wants to be sealed (off) from the world. Like put it in a bubble and put it in orbit around the earth and I think that would make them happier than anything else because then they couldn't be reached by anyone. Then it's affluent to a degree that's somewhat exaggerated in the minds of others. There are some very (poor) citizens. There are some who make it with the help of food stamps and just manage to make it on their social security. But if that is so, it's considered shameful, and they sneak into Jonesville or into Missionville to do their shopping so that the food stamps are not seen. Many of them, I have my own theories regarding human beings, regarding retirement, I don't think that everybody can retire. The really stupid people, or let's say the less bright, cannot retire because they do not know what to do with their leisure time. This requires a little imagination and it requires a zest for living which is noticably absent (here)...

What of the problem of isolation among High Heaven

residents? This feeling was rampant here as well and for many of the same reasons. For example, while High Heaven residents had easy access to intracity and intercity transportation, there were factors mitigating against its use. With regard to intercity transportation, the greatest constraint was lack of income. High Heaven residents did not have sufficient funds to go on outings or extended vacations. Poor health constrained other would-be travelers, and for six months a year poor weather was a serious hindrance. Another factor turned on the question of security. Residents rarely left the building during the evening hours for fear of muggings, and left in groups or only reluctantly by themselves during the daytime. While it is true High Heaven had shopping, church lunches and volunteer functions that were only a few blocks away and within easy walking distance (there was also a free pick-up service for many of these activities), they became inaccessable a good part of the year when freezing temperatures and the ice and snow made even a trip to the market two blocks away a hazardous proposition. Few residents left the building during the winter months, and then only when visitors came to take them out on weekends.

In short, while transportation was available to High Heaven residents, its usage was restricted by lack of funds, poor health, poor weather and problems of security. These were some of the most prevalent external and natural constraints upon travel that worked to limit the extent and nature of interaction between the residents themselves and the residents and greater community.

There were also, as in the case of Fun City, self-limiting factors. The preceding chapter explained how many High Heaven residents were by choice social isolates. They were not active in in-house activities or clubs, they sought to avoid the gossip mill, they watched a lot of television and, generally, they kept to themselves. There was then a tremendous apathy among High Heaven and Fun City residents. We discussed in the last chapter the general reluctance of High Heaven residents to interact not only with students, but among themselves and with the greater community.

In fact, Fun City and High Heaven both required of their residents a high level of self-motivation. Other residents did little to actively recruit members into existing cliques or formal organizations. Unfortunately, very few of Fun City's or High Heaven's residents were "self-actualized"* persons. One very active Fun City resident aptly summed up this dilemma,

> And I think that (the developer) who built this place (Fun City), if ever they build a monument to him, I'm willing to give a quarter toward it. This (Fun City) fills my needs. Now, I know other people who are very unhappy here, but you see, we need to keep busy, and that's the secret of being contented. You must do something . . . not on the go physically because we're not able to. In fact I find it necessary to use a cane when I'm walking, but still and all, mentally, if you don't do something, if you just sit on your chair and watch the idiot box here day after day, if you just do nothing (you'll be very unhappy). I know people who have been here for years and they don't know what to do. People with money, fairly intelligent people, very successful people, but here they are at a loss.

To the extent that the residents of both populations were subject to the above constraints, there were many socially isolated and unhappy people in these settings. There was one factor that worked to soften this hardship for High Heaven residents, and that was their greater phone and personal contact with locally-based relatives and old friends. While the extent of contact varied from resident to resident from no outside contact to almost daily phone or direct contact, this feature of High Heaven living was a definite asset in promoting and sustaining meaningful forms of interaction with others.

In short, it was not so much their relocation to the unique retirement setting that High Heaven offered that resulted in a happy retirement situation for the residents, but rather, for many, it was their continued contact with a familiar past that helped mollify the negative effects of their unfamiliar present.

Mr. S.: Yeah, I worked until I was seventy-two (as a cabinet maker). My eightieth birthday I quit, I quit working. (Between 72 and 80 Mr. S. worked part time and did odd jobs.) I thought it was about time to quit then. I've enjoyed every day of it. I've got four children of my own,

---

*For a discussion of self-actualized persons, see Abraham Mazlow, *Toward a Psychology of Being, New York, Van Nostand Reinhold, 1968.*

fourteen grandchildren and ten great grandchildren spread all the way from Hawaii to (upstate New York).

Dr. J.: How many live here?

Mr. S.: Well, I got my two sons living here and all the grandchildren and my great grandchildren. There's about fourteen or fifteen lives right here (in town).

Dr. J.: Do you see your children a lot?

Mr. S.: Oh, yes, my son comes in and has lunch with me every noon. Once a week he comes in and picks me up on Sunday afternoon and we all go out to (a suburb) to be there with his family, and next Sunday I'll go to my other son's. They keep me occupied. I enjoy it; that's what makes me so young.

Planned Social Activities

We discussed in the preceding chapter the relative lack of planned social activities at High Heaven compared to Fun City. It was also noted how resident apathy and the effects of the gossip mill tended to minimize residents' participation in these activities. This similarity between High Heaven and Fun City will now be considered in greater detail.

You will recall that Fun City had ninety-two clubs and formal organizations each of which boasted a high paper membership. The question was posed, how many actually participated in these activities? The answer is, very few. Fun City offered an excellent example of the fact that providing for an active social life in no way insured an active participation.

For example, the arts and crafts club listed a membership of 198 Fun City residents. It was open daily to members from 10:00 a.m. to 12:00 noon and from 1:00 to 3:00 p.m. A typical turnout for the arts and crafts clubs follows: ceramics club, 4-10; woodshop, 2-6; lapidary and jewelry shop, 2-6; art class, 0-8; and sewing class, 0-8. These figures, while a fair estimate of the extent of group activity in the arts and crafts clubs on a typical day, are somewhat deceiving. Other club members who did not actually attend the workshop settings took materials home to work on. However, while this provided them with a meaningful pastime, it did little to promote resident interaction or a sense of community.

Some of the more active clubs were better attended. This was probably a result of the better health among their members. For example, the bicycle club with 139 members typically had thirty to forty cyclists on an outing, while the square dance club with 250 members usually had from fifty to sixty members for square dancing on Wednesday night.

On the other hand, some active sports clubs had relatively poor participation. For example, it was previously noted that Fun City had a number of separate golf clubs with a combined membership of over 600 members. However, there were rarely more than fifty to seventy-five persons on the fairways on any one day. This was true partially because of the typically hot weather (most golfers were out and back before noon), and also because the Fun City course was only mediocre and relatively expensive to use. As a result, some residents actually drove to better and less expensive nearby courses to golf. This was ironic when so many had come to Fun City in the first place because of the promise of good inexpensive golf facilities.

If large physically active clubs were poorly attended, many large passive membership clubs were relatively well-attended. Prime among these were the card clubs. Playing cards in Fun City was second only to TV-watching

Dr. J.:   How about those people who aren't very active or even members of the clubs?

Mr. N. Well, television has made a lot of things possible that wasn't true with my father and my grandfather. Oftentimes I wonder about my grandfather who lived in a farm in Pennsylvania — What in the world he did with himself? Get up and work all day and evening came and he would eat, and uh, what did he do? He would go to bed on an old straw mattress. And, of course, they got up quite early. But gee, a life like that I just couldn't take. I think it would drive me nuts. I think television has been a great thing with shut-ins and people like that because they still have pretty good programs ... I watch it lots in the afternoon — different programs. *And we have cable (TV) in here, you know, where we get fine reception. And uh, oh it's one of these places that it would be hard to maintain, I think, without television. People would feel too isolated, too away from things. Regardless of the age you become you kind of want to get in the millstream a little bit you know.* (Emphasis added) So with television and radio, at night when I've slept too much in the daytime I have a radio by my bed. I have an ear thing, and I put that between my pillows and I listen to that all night long — the news, you know. So, what's the difference? I might just as well listen to that. I don't care if I sleep or not. It doesn't make any difference. Sometimes I get up. I have one of those recliner chairs, and I sit in that and read and fall asleep and maybe sleep there for a couple of hours. What difference does it make? I've accomplished nothing down here... There's a few people in the evening (out for a walk) like my wife — my wife walks the dog in the evening. I walk her in the daytime, and there's a few couples out that you meet, you know, that like to walk in the cool of the evening, *but most of them are glued to their television.* (Emphasis added)

Without going into a breakdown of the extent of participation in each of Fun City's planned social clubs and organizations, a fair summary would be that there is generally a large paper membership but small participating membership in these clubs, and that those clubs promoting a passive way of life are generally better attended than those promoting an active way of life. Quite apart from the number of activities available to Fun City residents, which far outnumbered those offered at High Heaven, the general apathy described above was equally binding in both settings.

Political and Ethnic Orientations

Another unanticipated similarity between Fun City and High Heaven residents was their political conservatism and high echelon racism. This is peculiar in many regards. After all, Fun City residents were formerly employed as professionals, white collar workers or skilled laborers while High Heaven residents were recruited primarily from the ranks of unskilled labor. Fun City residents were recruited primarily from the upper or upper middle class cosmopolitan environment of the metropolis while High Heaven residents came primarily from low or middle income neighborhoods of small towns. Fun City residents were relatively well-educated while many High Heaven residents never graduated from high school.

How was it, then, that these polar opposites in SES terms were so similar in their political and ideological leanings? For example, we indicated in the preceding chapter the negative feelings many High Heaven residents held toward *hippies, welfare-types,* dropouts, blacks, *Communists* and other marginal members of society. That some were themselves currently on welfare, were themselves black or had previously led colorful lives in no way diminished their rancor toward such persons. This was true of Fun City residents as well. We have already noted how Fun City's few politically liberal-minded citizens found it difficult or impossible, notwithstanding their every effort to get along, to meaningfully relate to many of their conservative neighbors or the townfolk in general. Some indication of this political conservatism is reflected in the *Fun City News.* The following examples are illustrative:

On Industry. American business is under attack. If the attack succeeds, the business system which has produced this country's prosperity will be destroyed or seriously impaired. Unfortunately, there is no sign of a major counterattack by free enterprise forces.

A hate-business climate is developing rapidly. Ralph Nader's continuing campaign against business has contributed substantially to this climate. The Nader reports have been published in pocketbook form, and are available on book racks around the country. Mr. Nader also lectures widely and appears frequently on TV. His charges and complaints go virtually unanswered...

The United States corporation represents the constructive force in the nation — the doers. Thus, it is under attack from the liberal-left ideologues and from the talkers who speak glibly of radically restructuring American society...

Business must speak out and explain how the hate-the-corporation attitude is destructive of the comfortable life enjoyed by the American people.

On Unionism. What can be done (to curb union monopoly power)? Efforts must be stepped up to curb the unions and to make them subject to antitrust laws. The public must insist that the government stop rewarding welfare and food stamp parasites who, in effect, loot our society. Moochers must be put to work. Every working man or woman in this country must make an effort to increase productivity to offset the high wage scales. The courts must strike down union rules which forbid productivity increases.

These changes are essential if American industry is to survive and the Pittsburghs of America are to retain their economic vitality.

On Environment. Repercussions from the disastrous vote on the SST (Supersonic Transport) in Congress last week continues to be heard from many sectors of the economy, and it is my educated guess that things will get worse before they get better for those who helped deal this cruel blow to the aerospace industry, one half of which is situated in Southern California.

Top victors in the weird struggle which resulted in demise of the SST by certain politicians have been the love children on their perennial ecology crusade at the expense of American science and technology which they have linked emotionally to the military-industrial complex.

What really won over the thinking of those who voted against the SST on Capitol Hill? Most likely, not the arguments usually cited ... but a cold calculating eye on the eighteen-year-old vote, the hippies, the youthful voices who have made the ecology their number one concern at the expense of American strength on the world stage and the domestic front at home.

On Hippies. One of the distinctive features of the 1970's is an inward-turning attitude on the part of many Americans.

On the lunatic fringe there is the phenomenon of the urban or rural commune where young people experiment in group living without formalities or responsibilities. Strange new cults flourish in some of our major cities.

Working citizens can't be expected to carry the hippie elements on their backs for years on end. There's no moral obligation on good citizens to subsidize or protect these people who won't accept any of the burdens or responsibilities of a person living in society.

In the last few years our country has gone on a binge of toleration insofar as irresponsible people are concerned. It is time to insist on a new measure of social discipline and respect for public authority.

It is time to demand that those who want to look inward and avoid the realities be brought face to face with the requirements of citizenship. The hip cultists can't be permitted to disrupt and spoil our society.

Part and parcel with this political conservatism was the covert racism that was true of so many Fun City and High Heaven residents. This feature of High Heaven living was discussed in the preceding chapter. While racism in High Heaven was rather straightforward, it took a curious turn in Fun City. In one sense there was no racism in Fun City. Indeed it has been previously noted that there were no blacks and few ethnics of any kind in Fun City to discriminate against. While there were no blacks living in Fun City proper, it was ironic that Fun City should have been located so near Jonesville. However, there were basic ecological and social differences between High Heaven and Fun City with regard to its proximity to the ghetto. Not only did blacks actually reside in High Heaven, but the black ghetto was only a block away. Ghetto residents shopped at the High Heaven market, and ghetto children sometimes played on High Heaven property. Indeed, one had only to look out his apartment window to see the ghetto and its residents. None of this was true in the case of Fun City.

Jonesville was located three or four miles away from Fun City and was separated from it by a kind of open, undeveloped wasteland. The residents of Jonesville rarely ever came to Fun City. A few shopped at the Fun City supermarkets, but were never seen out of the shopping center area and in the town proper, and Fun City residents never went to Jonesville. In fact, unless one population actively sought out the other (something neither did), they could spend a lifetime in adjacent towns and never see each other. Indeed, this is exactly how things were during the span of the study.

While the residents of Fun City did not live among or even see blacks within their community, they did resent the people of Jonesville and the idea that they were, in a sense, neighbors. Indeed, the fact that there were no blacks residing in Fun City was more than a happy coincidence for the white middle and upper class homeowners who lived there, and preferred to retire "among their own kind."*

How can the political parallels that existed between two apparently divergent populations be explained? One explanation hinges upon their ideological outlooks; both sets of residents incorporated *Horatio Alger, pull yourself up by your bootstraps*-view of the world, notwithstanding the fact that most High Heaven residents have, by Fun City standards, not succeeded in this lifelong undertaking. From this perspective, "work makes life sweet" is taken to be more than an idle proverb or a description of a possible life-style. Rather, the world view incorporated in the "Protestant Ethic and Spirit of Capitalism,"† is seen as the *only* "right way" to personal, social and spiritual salvation.

Couple this notion to one that holds "those who want to work, can" and the unemployed, welfare-types, dropouts and hippies, all become immoral by definition. The individual is not faulted from this ideological perspective with respect to how well he succeeds, but only how hard he tries. The extent of failure is seen to result from a flaw in the individual as opposed to a flaw in society; the moochers need only pull themselves up by their bootstraps. A great many residents of Fun City and High Heaven held this view. Such a perspective was further reinforced by the fact that, notwithstanding their different backgrounds, both sets of residents had experienced the great depression. The author feels that this common experience and the myriad of others that are a part of growing up during the same historical period provide a better explanation of the current similarities in their life-styles than some more frequently invoked sociological indicators of life chance, e.g. SES. Indeed, it is not so surprising to find that the outlooks and actions of these two groups of retired

---

*For a more detailed discussion of this aspect, see the author's work on Fun City.
†Max Weber, *The Protestant Ethic and the Spirit of Capitalism*, New York. Charles Scribner's Sons, 1958.

persons had more in common than one might have first supposed given their long-standing "reciprocity of standpoints and relevances"* stemming from their having experienced the above and other key events.

---

*Alfred Schutz, *Collected Papers*, Vol. 1, The Problem of Social Reality. The Hague, Martinus Nkjhoff, 1962, p. 11.

MERRILL COURT: A CASE STUDY

WE have seen in Chapter I and II that one's long-awaited retirement does not always end by fulfilling a lifelong dream of *at last, doing what we always wanted to*. In fact, retirement within the two settings discussed thus far fell far short of this expectation. The residents of Fun City and High Heaven, while representing two very different retirement populations and life-styles, had, notwithstanding these differences, much in common. Pervasive in both was a sense of social and physical isolation, apathy and loneliness. The extent to which the planners had provided things to do to ease the residents' transition from a work life-style to a leisure life-style was no indication of the settings' success in fulfilling this goal. Most residents pursued a passive, not an active way of life.

The third and last case study to be considered below will be something of a departure in this regard. Here, the researcher, Arlie Hochschild, found in Merrill Court *The Unexpected Community*.*

SOME PRELIMINARY OBSERVATIONS

As a retirement setting Merrill Court had more in common with High Heaven than Fun City. Like High Heaven it is public housing for the elderly that was completed in 1965 and caters to low income persons of low educational achievement. Like High Heaven the rentals were inexpensive ($55.00 per month) and the housing was new. The residents here were also long-standing residents of the community whose annual income was less than $2800.00 per year for single persons and $3000.00 if married. Nearly all lived on welfare. Like High Heaven, Merrill Court was not as geographically isolated as Fun City. It also had relatively

_____

*Arlie Russel Hochschild, *The Unexpected Community*, Englewood Cliffs, Prentice Hall, 1973.

little in the way of planned social activities, at least compared to Fun City, and yet, unlike High Heaven or Fun City, there was an active participation by the residents in in-house social events.

Merrill Court residents, like those in High Heaven, moved there not for the social environment that their retirement setting offered, but for the cheap rent. Merrill Court and High Heaven were both small retirement communities, at least compared to Fun City. Finally, unlike High Heaven, Merrill Court had no blacks or Jews living there; in this regard it was more like Fun City. It had managed to somehow form an unexpected community.

Hochshild's book purports to show that "old people who live among other old people make more friends than old people who live among young people .... and why and how this happens."* That such a state of affairs is possible as a specific instance of the general proposition that "old people disengage under certain social conditions but not under others," the author is prepared to allow, but as a statement of a general state of affairs, the notion that old people make more friends when living among old people than young people is not supported by the author's findings. The residents of Fun City did not make more firends than those in High Heaven. In many ways the retired persons living in Fun City were more, not less, socially isolated than those in High Heaven, and the residents in both of these settings had, unlike those in Merrill Court, little sense of community.

The question arises, Why were the residents of Merrill Court able to establish and perpetuate a sense of community while those in High Heaven and Fun City were not? First and foremost, there was the question of health. Persons in poor health are less likely to be active than those in good health. Hochschild notes that among the forty-three residents of Merrill Court ... "nearly all were widows, in good health." This was not true in High Heaven or Fun City. The good health of Merrill Court residents certainly played an important part in their being able to form a community.

---

*Hochschild notes in this connection a series of studies of retirement settings that show that "According to virtually all the research on attitudes of residents in old age communities, they like living together with other older people."

The active in-house participation of Merrill Court residents may have resulted more from such factors as the number of persons involved and their distribution within their living space rather than in the kinds of persons residing there. For example, it would be easier for interaction to occur among the forty-three residents located with a five-story building at Merrill Court than among 420 residents in a twenty-one story high-rise at High Heaven or the 6000 residents distributed one or two to each home in the sprawling tracked home community of Fun City.

Some indication of how the design of the building at Merrill Court affected the potential for interaction is given by Hochschild in the following description,

> (Merrill Court) had five floors: a ground floor with one apartment and large Recreation Room for common use, and four other floors with ten apartments on each floor. There was an elevator midway between the apartments, and a long porch extended the length of all the apartments. It was nearly impossible to walk from any apartment to the elevator without being watched from a series of living-room windows that looked out onto the porch ... A woman who was sewing or watching television in her apartment could easily glance up through the window and see or wave to a passerby.*

Such an arrangement was completely absent in High Heaven. Each apartment door opened onto a central rectangular hallway with the elevators situated in the center of the rectangle. Apartment doors in High Heaven were always closed for security purposes, and the occupants of any one apartment could not see, nor were they likely to encounter, the occupants of any other apartment in the course of their comings and goings. This closed circuit arrangement and its guarantee of privacy were subverted somewhat during the summer months when the unbearable heat obliged residents to sometimes open their apartment doors in the hope of creating a breeze. This led to a greater amount of visiting and casual forms of interaction among High Heaven residents. The above is some indication that it was more than the bad weather that accompanied the winter season that led residents to speak of winters in High Heaven as bleak and depressing.

---

*Arlie Russel Hochschild, *The Unexpected Community*, Englewood Cliffs, Prentice Hall, 1973, p. 4.

The potential for interaction at Merrill Court was further enhanced by the lack of physical and self-imposed constraints encountered in High Heaven and Fun City. In addition, there was, for Merrill Court, the researcher's own active role in transforming the setting into the community she describes, "Thus, I entered Merrill Court in 1966 to work for three summers and parts of three years, initially not as a sociologist but as an assistant recreation director."* She also served as a reporter for the *Merrill Court Gazette,* a monthly newsletter that she ". . . began to edit when I first started working" (at Merrill Court). This is an important intervening variable in any discussion of life-styles at Merrill Court, one that Hochschild has not dealt with. The question arises, To what extent was her participation as reporter and assistant program director responsible for creating a self-fulfilling prophecy? Did the residents generate and actively participate in all of the meaningful social interactions the study describes, or were these generated as they were at High Heaven during the golden era by talented and active outside third parties? It has been shown how it was possible to generate an active in-house participation in High Heaven with the assistance of the coordinator of social services and students, but that the residents themselves were incapable, of their own accord, of initiating and sustaining such activities. In this regard it is worthy of note that none of the many clubs and social activities Fun City had to offer were staffed by outside professionals. They were all manned by in-house volunteer residents. Of course, the outside intervention of third parties in no way guaranteed the active participation of residents. Already noted was the ineffective role of the second coordinator in the case of High Heaven. However, it does seem that the intervention of outsider movers was a necessary if not sufficient condition for generating active participation in in-house activities, and it is suggested that the researcher may herself have played such a role in the case of Merrill Court.

Finally, the author feels that Hochschild inferred a greater sense of involvement from the activities she described than the descriptions themselves seem to allow, although the implications

---

*Arlie Russel Hochschild, *The Unexpected Community,* Englewood Cliffs, Prentice Hall, 1973, p. 3.

she drew from her study are, like all others, subject to interpretation. The author's interpretation was that while there was more going on at Merrill Court than the researcher first supposed, there was not as much going on there as she was led to believe. If this is true, one could be led to overcompensate in this way. Upon first entering Fun City the author saw it as a living graveyard. The sense of *nothing is happening* constituting the typical *nothing unusual is happening* of this setting hits the observer like a ton of bricks. It is only through prolonged observation and becoming acquainted with the residents and what they know that one finds that there's more going than meets the eye. At this juncture it is easy to overcompensate and make more of it than it warrants. The author is unsure if Hochschild is guilty of this or not, but it is his impression that there is an element of this in her work. For these reasons and others to be considered later in this chapter, the author is reluctant to accept the notion that the elderly make more friends when living among the elderly than among the young or the general population at large. Not only does the author's research not support this position, but it is unclear to him how Hochschild's does either.

PLANNED SOCIAL EVENTS: DOWNSTAIRS AT MERRILL COURT*

The weekly social calendar at Merrill Court scheduled about twenty separate social events for its forty-three residents, while the weekly social calendar at Fun City listed about 120 events for 6000 residents. In spite of this there were numerically nearly as many Merrill Court residents who routinely showed up at their planned activities, especially arts and crafts, as there were Fun City residents who showed up at theirs. Why was this true? For one thing, the reader is told that at Merrill Court "there was not only social pressure to keep active and involved, but to be proper." While there was a great deal of social pressure at Fun City to be proper, and propriety was to a lesser extent a feature of High Heaven living, there was little if any pressure in either Fun City or

---

*Arlie Russel Hochschild, *The Unexpected Community*, Englewood Cliffs, Prentice Hall, 1973, p. 47.

High Heaven to keep active and involved. This aspect was discussed in some detail in the preceding chapters. Those who were not among the self-actualized were left to their own devices, which nearly always resulted in their social isolation and unhappiness. If outside or in-house social pressure is required to motivate others to become active participants in their available social environments, why did the residents of Merrill Court succeed in this so well while those in High Heaven and Fun City failed so badly?

It has already been suggested that Merrill Court may have had not only in-house pressure to be active, but outside assistance as well, i.e. the researcher who was also acting social director. There were other differences that predisposed Merrill Court to a more active social life. The author has discussed in a previous work the role of paid and volunteer work in Fun City and what it meant for the residents to be meaningfully, if not gainfully, employed. Hochschild notes how many of the activities comprising Merrill Court social life were defined by the participants as work, notwithstanding the outsiders' common sense appraisal of these activities as play, hobbies, or time-killers.

This was not true in Fun City or High Heaven. Most of their leisure time activities were taken to be hobbies, playtime pursuits or just ways to kill time. Card-playing, TV-watching, knitting, gossiping, bingo, arts and crafts, or volunteer efforts, all fell in this category. There were, of course, some activities defined by High Heaven and Fun City participants as work, e.g. shopping (which was also considered as social outing time), housecleaning, planning for and conducting holiday parties, holding an annual bazaar or occasional bake sale, helping sick friends or neighbors, or doing odd jobs for friends or neighbors either for pay, barter or returned favors. However, in Fun City and High Heaven nearly all formal or downstairs activities were seen as leisure time pursuits, while some "upstairs"* activities were seen as work, or at least work-related.

To the extent that work centered activities held greater

---

*Arlie Russel Hochschild, *The Unexpected Community*, Englewood Cliffs, Prentice Hall, 1973, p. 49.

importance in all three settings, and the tenants at Merrill Court defined more of their activities as work-related, this probably helped contribute to the greater active participation that Hochschild noted.

It is difficult in such an analysis to separate the chicken from the egg, that is, it is not clear whether the work definition of the situation held by so many Merrill Court residents contributed to their more active participation in collective activities, which in turn provided the potential for creating the unexpected community, or whether the sense of community preceded these collective efforts and was responsible for them. In all likelihood there was a reciprocal effect.

Some of the reasons why more Merrill Court residents may have been more actively engaged than Fun City or High Heaven residents have been considered, however, there may have been other contributing factors as well. For example, apart from their small number and physical proximity, Merrill Court residents were, judging from the case histories, even more homogeneous than those in High Heaven or Fun City. The effects of shared background expectancies in producing people better able to communicate with one another was noted at the conclusion of the last chapter. The exceptions to the realization of this greater potential for communication among persons from similar backgrounds would be the constraining effects of their social environments and/or shared background expectancies insofar as these, for whatever reasons, could be considered reasons to minimize interactions with others. Indeed, it has been previously noted how these two constraints operated to minimize meaningful interactions among Fun City and High Heaven residents, notwithstanding the relative homogeneity of their respective populations. By the same token, the absence of these two factors upon the social world by Merrill Court residents probably contributed in great measure to promoting the greater interaction that Hochschild describes.

The question arises, What sort of activities did the residents of Merrill Court engage in to promote meaningful forms of interactions? In large measure they were many of the same kind that were available at Fun City and High Heaven. As previously indicated, Hochschild divided social activities at Merrill Court into two basic categories, *upstairs* and *downstairs* activities. Downstairs activities are planned group activities, most of which participants tended to define as work. Upstairs activities were the kinds of informal interactions residents engaged in, such as visiting each other in their apartments, gossiping, watching TV or having coffee with a friend. A typical downstairs weekly calendar of events for Merrill Court is given below.* Hochschild offers it to indicate the extent of Merrill Court's active social life.

Monday	10:00	Service club meeting
	11:00	Pot luck lunch
	1:00	Workshop on church bazaar
	4:00	Tin class
Tuesday	10:00	Workshop
	1:00	Bowling league
	3:00	Visit Pine Manor Nursing Home
	4:00	Christmas party committee meeting
Wednesday	10:00	Workshop
	1:00	Social service committee meeting
	2:00	Birthday committee
	7:00	Bible class
Thursday	10:00	Workshop
	11:00	Bake sale, shopping plaza
	4:00	Bingo
Friday	10:00	Workshop
	12:00	Pot luck lunch
	2:00	Band practice
	5:30	Open supper

As previously noted, this list of events was in no way remarkable. It was only slightly longer than that usually posted in High Heaven, and did not begin to approach the extensive weekly list of scheduled events at Fun City. What was remarkable, according to Hochschild, was the extent of resident participation. However, the data needed to support this contention is conspicuously

---

*Arlie Russel Hochschild, *The Unexpected Community*, Englewood Cliffs, Prentice Hall, 1973, p. 1.

absent. While Hochschild provides rich descriptions of the activities and roles that developed at Merrill Court and their meanings to the participants, there is very little in the way of a simple head count to indicate the extent of participation. We are not informed how many of Merrill Court's forty-three residents typically attended the calendar of events noted above. This is difficult to understand, given Hochschild's otherwise scrupulous attention to details. There were some exceptions; for example, we are told "only eight were regular players" at the once-a-week "Recreation Day" activity called "Game Day." This figure was given to indicate how few Merrill Court residents were interested in games and how many defined their activities as work. It does not note how many were sometime players on games day, or why eight persons at games should be considered low attendance while thirteen persons attending a workshop described elsewhere should be considered high attendance. In another instance the reader is told that . . . "most of the residents and a half-dozen non-residents belonged . . ." to the Merrill Court Service Club. Quite apart from the question of how many was "most," i.e. how many did not belong, is the question of how many participated.

It was noted elsewhere that Fun City clubs had impressive membership lists but little active participation. In this regard it is difficult for the reader to get any firsthand information about the extent of participation in Merrill Court's downstairs activities apart from the researchers repeated assurance that ". . . Merrill Court was a beehive of activity." An observer of Fun City's clubs and memberships on a good day would come to a similar conclusion. Indeed, newspaper reporters from other cities visiting Fun City for a human interest story invariably reported Fun City to be a beehive of activity. For the 500 active residents who were routinely involved in planned and informal social events centering about the activity center, it was. However, this said nothing of the remaining 5,500 residents who did not participate in these activities and were literally nowhere to be seen. This is not meant to imply that this was true of Merrill Court, but rather that the data presented in the study offers insufficient information for drawing any conclusions one way or the other.

INFORMAL SOCIAL NETWORK:
UPSTAIRS AT MERRILL COURT

How downstairs activities at Merrill Court were much like those at High Heaven has already been covered. The critical difference between them was the greater participation and social involvement of Merrill Court residents; the same was true of upstairs events.

However, there was even a greater similarity in life-styles between the two with respect to upstairs living. Not only were there a greater number of the same activities, but there was a greater involvement by High Heaven residents in informal forms of interactions. While the extent of informal interactions at High Heaven did not match that at Merrill Court, it was closer than in the case of planned social events. Let us consider some of these similarities. Hochschild notes,

> Neighboring is also a way to detect sickness or death ... The widows in good health took it upon themselves to care for one or two in poor health ... Even those who had not adopted someone to help often looked after a neighbor's potted plants while they were visiting kin, lent kitchen utensils, and took phone messages. One woman wrote letters for those who "wrote a poor hand."[*]

These kinds of courtesies towards one's neighbors were a part of High Heaven living as well. In Chapter II well tenants caring for sick ones, bringing them food on occasion or shopping for them was noted. However, while some neighbors extended these courtesies willingly, others came to resent having to do this on a routine basis. This was not surprising when one realizes that there were more sick persons at High Heaven than at Merrill Court, and that, unlike Merrill Court, High Heaven had a public health facility in the building that residents believed should have been responsible for caring for the increasing number of ailing tenants. Like Merrill Court, High Heaven also invoked the practice of checking to see if neighbors were all right. In fact this procedure was institutionalized. Apart from the automatic alarm system in each apartment, there were two floor representatives per

---

[*]Arlie Russel Hochschild, *The Unexpected Community*, Englewood Cliffs, Prentice Hall, 1973, p. 53.

floor in High Heaven whose duties were to make sure everything was all right. This was quite apart from the more informal dropping in on neighbors or the workings of the gossip mill that served the same purpose. Many of the above features were true at Fun City as well. One key difference was that the tenants of Merrill Court (more so than those of High Heaven or Fun City) were less reticent in welcoming uninvited guests. This, too, went a long way toward promoting meaningful forms of interaction.

Another similarity between High Heaven and Merrill Court was that while one might drop in to chat, gossip or have a cup of coffee, one rarely invited others for dinner. It was previously noted that High Heaven residents also drew the line at breaking bread with neighbors in that this incurred an obligation and inferred a sense of closeness that residents sought to avoid. Hochschild refers to this aspect of Merrill Court living as follows,

> There was a distinction between socializing over a cup of coffee and socializing over a meal. As Irma commented, "Sometimes I see Rosy in the elevator and she says, 'Come on over for a cup of coffee, or else she calls and I shuffle over in my housecoat and slippers." But she added, "There's a problem, when you invite a person to lunch, you can't know where to stop."*

The above offers one interesting common denominator to High Heaven, Merrill Court and Fun City living. Hochschild, having noted this occurence, does not pursue it. For the author's part, he can only wonder why. It is, after all, peculiar. Among friends in the outside world, there is nothing unusual about inviting another to dinner. Indeed, it is one way of reaffirming that a friendship exists. Why was it, then, that at Merrill Court, where a sense of community was supposed to be so strong, it was unheard of, and for the same reason that it was not done in High Heaven or Fun City where there was little sense of community. In these settings everyone wanted to be friendly, but not too friendly. At least as important as not giving offence was keeping one's distance. The latter is a practice the author does not associate with building strong friendships or a sense of community. Here again, one can only wonder if Hochschild did not perhaps infer a

---

*Arlie Russel Hochschild, *The Unexpected Community*, Englewood Cliffs, Prentice Hall, 1973, p. 51.

stronger sense of togetherness than actually existed.

Another common denominator in these three retirement settings that was associated more with upstairs than downstairs living was related to the general concept of relative deprivation. There was a tendency for active tenants to feel sorry for inactive ones; both the active and inactive felt sorry for those recuperating from an illness, while those recuperating from an illness felt sorry for the hospitalized, and all of the above felt sorry for those they perceived as terminal cases and who had been moved to nursing homes. This informal rating system operated in High Heaven, Fun City, and Hochschild notes its existence in Merrill Court as well, "Those in politics and recreation referred to the passive card players and newspaper readers as 'poor dears.' Old people with passive lifestyles in good health referred to those in poor health as 'poor dears' and those in poor health but living in independent housing referred to those in nursing homes as 'Poor Dears.' "*

Another feature of upstairs living relates to the nature of interaction networks. Hochschild notes that, "Most neighbors were also friends, and friendships, as well as information about them, were mainly confined to each floor ... † All but four (tenants) had their best friends on the same floor and only a few had a next-best friend on another floor." This pattern of interaction was somewhat modified at High Heaven; while tenants tended to know most about what went on on their floor, many had best friends located on other floors. Picking one's floor was something over which one had no control. This was further complicated by the turnover in population that changed the resident make-up of each floor, sometimes radically, and over a brief span of time. As a result, the residents of High Heaven referred to *good floors* and *bad floors*. Good floors were those that contained few alcoholics, sick persons or otherwise troublesome neighbors. In this regard the higher floors of High Heaven tended to be better floors, the lower ones, worst. This was true not only because of the chance assignments of persons or the natural

---

*Arlie Russel Hochschild, *The Unexpected Community*, Englewood Cliffs, Prentice Hall, 1973, p. 60.
†Arlie Russel Hochschild, *The Unexpected Community*, Englewoodk Cliffs, Prentice Hall, 1973. p. 51.

history of the building, but because the housing authority tended to assign the lower floors to more disabled residents. As a consequence, tenants sometimes perceived that they lived on bad floors while their friends lived on good ones.

One's best friends might, of course, live on the same floor. Then, too, the residents of the same floor interacted (to one extent or another) with one another, independent of friendships, but it was not true of High Heaven as it was of Merrill Court that best friends were recruited mainly from the same floor or even that information about them was necessarily confined to the same floor.

Yet another similarity between Merrill Court, High Heaven and Fun City was the notion of *age, the leveler*. Hochschild notes, "The masses more often mention the fact of age, which democratized the group. For example, as Mrs. Farmer frequently brought out, 'We're all elder people here. The club president isn't a day younger than any of us. There's no reason for her to be feeling so special.'"* This aspect of retirement living was true at High Heaven and Fun City as well. It was particularly so in Fun City where the discrepancies between the former statuses of residents was frequently striking. While Fun City residents were usually from upper middle or upper class backgrounds, the social distance between a millionaire (and there were several in Fun City) and a life-long civil servant or skilled laborer was greater than one would expect to find among the public housing residents of High Heaven or Merrill Court. However, in a formal sense, the feature of *age, the leveler* worked in a similar manner in all three settings.

SIBLING AND PARENT-CHILD BONDS

A subset of the notion of equality is what Hochschild refers to as "sibling bonds" as opposed to "parent-child" bonds.† The former she defines in terms of two basic features, "(1) reciprocity, and (2) similarity between two people. Reciprocity implies equality; what you do for me I return to you in equal measure."

---

*Arlie Russel Hochschild, *The Unexpected Community*, Englewood Cliffs, Prentice Hall, 1973, p. 57.

This as opposed to "parent-child bonds" which are not "based upon reciprocity or similarity. What you do for me I cannot return in equal measure. I depend on you more than you depend on me. And what is exchanged is different, not similar."

To illustrate this point Hochschild lists a number of activities such as "... the custom of exchanging cups of coffee, lunches, potted plants ..." However, as noted earlier, residents, while they exchanged cups of coffee, did not exchange lunches, and that omission of this practice was characteristic not only of Merrill Court, but High Heaven as well. In fact, insofar as breaking bread is symbolically taken to infer the features Hochschild refers to under "sibling bonds," it is an event that is conspicuously absent from Merrill Court living and may be taken as a counterinstance of the operation of sibling bonds. Hochschild notes that,

> Not all groups of old people form this sibling-bond — for example, old people in institutions (such as hospitals or nursing homes) do not ... *There is clearly something different between institutions and public housing apartments* ... The resident of the institution is "a patient." Like a child, he has his meals served to him, his water glass filled, his bed made, his blinds adjusted by his "mother nurse." He cannot return the favor."*(Emphasis added)

The question arises, Why at High Heaven, another public housing facility for older persons, was there so little in the way of sibling bonds? Why was it even more rare in Fun City? Neither of these settings were subject to the constraints of institutional living, and High Heaven, especially, had much in common with Merrill Court. The answer to this question has, at least in part, already been discussed. Basically it has two parts. First, there may not have been a Merrill Court as much in the way of sibling bonds as Hochschild believes. Her own accounts, the author feels, leave at least room for doubt. Secondly, it has already been discussed in this chapter why there would be a greater potential for the development of sibling bonds at Merrill Court than at High Heaven or Fun City, and it is likely that this potential was to some extent realized.

---

*For the discussion of sibling bonds and parent-child bonds that follows, see Hochschild, *Ibid.* p. 64 & 65.

In this sense, the author does not question Hochschild's contention that there were more meaningful relationships at Merrill Court (characterized by sibling bonds) than were found at High Heaven or Fun City. However, he does question whether or not they were as pervasive as Hochschild suggests, and more important, *whether age-stratified retirement settings are likely to produce such bonds, while nonage-stratified settings are not.* The author's own research does not allow for such a conclusion. Granting that sibling bonds were formed among some of the residents of Fun City and High Heaven, and, indeed, they are formed to one extent or another among persons in a wide range of social settings, one could not say of High Heaven or Fun City that the patterns or interaction there were characterized by sibling bonds — they were not.

Nor did it seem to be the case in the author's research that "Old people living among peers are much less likely to be disengaged, to isolate themselves, or to be isolated." The fact is that the residents of High Heaven were least disengaged, and the least isolated during the golden era or student-resident interaction. It was also during that period that they seemed more engaged and less isolated than the residents of Fun City who lived exclusively among their peers. With this in mind, the fact that Merrill Court residents were able to form the unexpected community that Hochschild describes is no indication that age-segregated communities are, per se, preferable social settings for establishing a sense of community. In some circumstances they may be; in others they may not.

To sum up this section by turning a phrase Hochschild uses to argue against the notion of "disengagement,"

> There is a well-known theory in gerontology called the theory of disengagement. According to it, as people grow older, they reduce their ties to the outside world and invest less emotion in the ties they retain. In doing so they gradually "die" socially before they die biologically. This process, according to the theory, is "natural" ... *My own field work suggests that this describes nothing "natural" but merely what happens under certain social conditions. Old people living among peers are much less likely to disengage, to isolate themselves, or to be*

isolated.* (Emphasis added)

The author believes that the contention contained in the last line, which Hochschild holds as a critique of *disengagement theory,* can be turned against her own work. There is nothing natural about the sense of community and the degree of engagement she describes in Merrill Court. Whether or not older persons living among their peers are more or less likely to disengage is itself contingent upon certain social conditions. These have been considered in some detail in the discussions of Fun City and High Heaven.

---

*Arlie Russel Hochschild, *The Unexpected Community,* Englewood Cliffs, Prentice Hall, 1973, p. 68.

Chapter IV

SOME THEORETICAL IMPLICATIONS

How do the case studies contained in this volume relate to the broader theoretical issues of aging? Unfortunately, as things now stand, there is little social theory to be found in the gerontological literature. There is, however, a plethora of *armchair speculation*, recommendation and advice regarding the clinical and social problems of older persons.

Probably the most publicized, popularized and criticized theory of aging, is Cumming and Henry's "Disengagement" model.* This position holds that, with growing age, people tend to disengage both socially and emotionally, and they become less constrained by what others think of them while in the pursuit of greater enjoyment. A further contention is that this disengagement is functionally beneficial not only for the individual, but for society.

Hochschild deals at some length with the disengagement hypothesis (treated by theory in the literature) as it relates to her own findings. However, most of this discussion is not found in her book, *The Unexpected Community*, but in her doctoral dissertation. As a result, the following discussion, when referring to her work, will be referring primarily to her dissertation. The author wants to pursue this aspect of her work and his own, not because the disengagement theory of aging requires one more critique, but because, given the literature in gerontology, the ethnographic case studies contained in this volume provide a unique basis for such a critique and a starting point for grounded theory. Existing critiques are different in that they are based upon different sources of data and are subject to different forms of analysis. These may be seen as falling into five basic categories,

1. survey research mailed or directly administered questionnaire studies dealing primarily with respondents' attitudes

---

*Elaine Cumming and William Henry, *Growing Old: The Process of Disengagement*, New York, Basic Books, 1961.

117

2. one-shot interview studies, i.e. a large number of researchers descend en masse on a community, and over a short span of time, interview and/or observe a number of persons
3. demographic studies concerned with changing large-scale social trends, e.g. age pyramids, geographic distribution of the aged, changing health or work patterns, etc.
4. clinical studies (psychological and social dimensions of aging in institutional settings usually interpreted within some therapeutic model)
5. theoretical studies based upon the findings of any or all of the above and/or armchair speculation.

Conspicuously absent from the above sources of data, which could serve both as a foundation for theory-building and a basis for critique, is detailed descriptive material based upon informal interviews and direct observations conducted over time of older persons in their natural environments. In short, field studies are needed that not only describe behavioral events but provide the reader with member's knowledge regarding the meanings of these acts as experienced by the actors at the time and in the social situations in which they occurred. With the almost complete absence of this kind of data from the gerontological literature it is perhaps not surprising to find precious little theory or, perhaps more important, a way of formulating theoretical positions so that they are given to *empirical disproof.*

With this in mind let us consider now how the data in the preceding three case studies relate to gerontology's most popular theory of aging, the disengagement model.

In her dissertation, Hochschild relates the findings of her study of Kidd Manor (Merrill Court) to four basic assumptions of the disengagement hypothesis, i.e. persons with increasing age become
1. socially disengaged
2. psychologically (emotionally) disengaged
3. less concerned for what others think of them or their behavior, i.e. are subject to desocialization and a lessening of normative control
4. more concerned with pursuing enjoyment and less with pursuing achievement.

Hochschild finds that the residents of Merrill Court do not live up to any of these expectations of the disengagement model and concludes, therefore, that they were not disengaged. It is further held that it is not age per se that leads to disengagement in later life, but the social setting one is a part of during this stage of the life cycle. Since she found the residents of Merrill Court to be very much engaged, Hochschild contends that age-graded retirement settings are preferable to those not graded by age for encouraging engagement. The author has already indicated why his own findings do not support this contention. To him it seems that it is not a question of age-graded retirement settings or those not graded by age that tends to enhance the extent of engagement among older persons. Rather, it is the particular social conditions to be found in either of these settings that is responsible for their success or failure in promoting an active and meaningful way of life for the residents.

With respect to the first two points noted above, many of the residents in High Heaven and Fun City were socially and psychologically disengaged. On these points the author's findings are at odds with Hochschild's and he has previously examined some of the reasons for this discrepancy and offered some explanations for it. The author has noted and tried to explain why other residents of High Heaven and Fun City (a small minority) were actively engaged. These explanations turned upon a discussion of certain social conditions found in these settings.

However, with respect to the remaining two points, i.e. the lessening concern with the opinions of others, and the decreasing emphasis on achievement and the increasing emphasis on enjoyment, Hochschild's findings tend to coincide with the author's. Contrary to the expectations of the disengagement model, the residents of Fun City and High Heaven, like those of Merrill Court, were very much concerned with their neighbors' opinions of them, and like the residents of Merrill Court, but to a lesser extent, many were still concerned with achievement. The way in which this concern manifested itself was discussed in some detail in Chapters II and III. In short, the author would agree with Hochschild's findings regarding the last two features of the disengagement model, for these conditions were not met in Fun City or High Heaven either, although the discrepancy was less sharply drawn there than at Merrill Court.

Using ethnographic data, the author has shown elsewhere how a critique of disengagement can be expanded in other directions. For example, Rose, in outlining the key features of the disengagement model, notes that, " ... the society and the individual prepare in *advance* for the ultimate 'disengagement' of incurable, incapacitating disease and death by *an inevitable, gradual and mutually satisfying process of disengagement from society.*"* (Emphasis added) The author has shown in his study, *Fun City,* that the residents comprised four basic categories of retired persons,†

1. engaged in the preretirement and postretirement period
2. disengaged in the preretirement and postretirement period
3. formerly engaged dropouts
4. the disengaged.

It was shown that the first three categories of persons, representing approximately half of the resident population, did not fit the conditions of the disengagement model as given above. It was further noted that while those in category 4 did seem to fit the model to the extent that they were disengaged and had prepared *in advance* for the disengagement and were *satisfied with it,* it was not clear even here that the disengagement was either *inevitable, gradual* or mutually beneficial either for the residents or society.

The author wishes to note at this point what the reader is probably by now well aware of, i.e. it is not easy to explain the differences and similarities between these three settings. However, first and foremost, it is important to recognize their existence. The above case studies are helpful in this regard. The author is aware that the discrepancies outlined above and the lack of pat answers for explaining them tend to muddy the waters. However it is essential that the social sciences come to recognize

---

*Arnold M. Rose, A Current Theoretical Issue in Social Gerontology, *Gerontologist,* 4:46-50, 1965.

†For a more detailed account of this aspect, see Jerry Jacobs, *Fun City: An Ethnographic Study of a Retirement Community,* New York, Holt, Rinehart and Winston, 1974.

and admit the complexity of social interactions and the fact that systematic and parsimonious explanations are not easily come by. Those who have undertaken the search are painfully aware of this, the many social theories to be found in the literature notwithstanding. The author believes the move toward a social science would proceed with greater dispatch if more researchers recognized and openly acknowledged this problem. He also believes it might be well for the discipline to begin at the beginning and do as so many have repeatedly recommended — first observe, describe and categorize social events, then construct theories to fit the data. It is ironic that those who most recommend the pursuit of such a program in the name of social science have least abided by it, and are first to chide those who have. Such studies should be encouraged and require no apology to those who contend that field studies offer only discriptions. Without such descriptive data to build upon, and there is precious little of it to be found in the literature, theories of social behavior are likely to prove (as they repeatedly have) to be only theories. The theory of disengagement as it relates to aging is one of these.

The ethnographic case studies of retirement settings given in this volume, while they do not provide all the answers to the questions the material generate, do provide some. One very basic finding is that such studies are not necessarily parochial, and the data can be applied to larger theoretical issues. The author has demonstrated this potential of ethnographic studies in previous works as well.*

A second major point is that it may be more fruitful to consider not so much the merits of this or that kind of retirement setting, but the pattern of social interaction *within* these various settings. Ultimately, it is the form and extent of interaction and not the kind of setting that generates engagement or disengagement among the participants. The patterns of interaction, in turn, while they are partially influenced by the constraints of the social structure, are also strongly affected by the particular characteristics of the participants. The patterns of interaction, then, within any given social setting, are problematic. These

---

*Jerry Jacobs, Symbolic Bureaucracy: A Case Study of a Social Welfare Agency, *Social Forces*, 47(4), June, 1969, pp. 413-433.

interaction patterns, while influenced by the social constraints of the immediate setting and parent system, are also influenced by the actions of the participants. Indeed, this influence is sometimes so radical as to change not only the patterns of interaction within the particular setting, but the parent system as well.

The author feels that sociology has and continues to pay insufficient attention to the particular actors that comprise social settings and puts undue stress upon the effects of the system and its capacity to shape behavior. It is abundantly clear that the acts of individuals have had a good deal to do with shaping the system, and that bureaucracy, notwithstanding its every effort, has not yet succeeded in ending the powerful influence of the charismatic man. Contemporary history is replete with examples. Weber's prophecy has not yet been realized, and it is unfortunate and perhaps ironic that sociology has prematurely abandoned not only the search for "verstehen", but the influence of charismatic leaders.

The above studies indicate that similar settings may produce very different interaction patterns and that this is best understood not only with reference to the kind of setting, but also with respect to special characteristics of the individuals comprising it. The individuals may, after all, vary independently of the kinds of settings, e.g. Merrill Court and High Heaven, and the ensuing differences in interaction patterns may be altered accordingly, the effects of "social facts" and *its all situational* notwithstanding.

The author suggests that field studies constitute an important and neglected perspective from which to study the reciprocal effects of social settings upon individuals, individuals upon social setting and the relationship of the resulting interactions to social structure. In this regard the studies presented in this volume offer some insight not only into the nature of retirement settings for older persons or a fruitful perspective from which to study other settings of this kind, but more generally give some appreciation for how such studies relate to the efforts of macrosociology and the central question of Hume; "How is society possible?"

BIBLIOGRAPHY

Albrecht, R.: Retirement hotels in Florida. In Osterbind, C.C. (Ed.): *Feasible Planning for Social Change in the Field of Aging.* University of Florida, Institute of Gerontology, Series 18. Gainsville, University of Florida Press, 1969.

Atchley, Robert C.: Retirement and leisure participation: Continuity of crisis? *Gerontologist, 11*:13, 1971.

——Retirement and work orientation. *Gerontologist, 11:*29, 1971.

Barfield, Richard, and Morgan, James: *Early Retirement: The Decision and the Experience.* Ann Arbor, Institute for Social Research, 1969.

Barker, M. B.: *California Retirement Communities.* Berkeley, The University of California Press, 1966.

Beckman, R. O.: The acceptance of congregated life in a retirement village. *Gerontologist, 9*:281, 1969.

Bennett, Ruth, and Lucille, Nahemow: Institutional totality and criteria of social adjustment in residences for the aged. *J Soc Issues, 21*:(4)44,

Beyer, Glenn, and Woods, Margaret E.: *Living and Activity Patterns of the Aged.* Research Report #6, Ithaca, New York, Center for Housing and Environmental Studies, Cornell University, 1963.

Beyer, Glenn: Living arrangements, attitudes and preferences of older people. In Tibbitts, C., and Donahue, W.: *Social and Psychological Aspects of Aging.* 1962, pp. 348-369.

Bixby, Lenore E., and Rings, E. Eleanor: Work experience of men claiming retirement benefits, 1966. *Social Security Bulletin, 32*:3, 1969.

Blau, Zena Smith: Structural constraints on friendship in old age. *Am Sociol Rev, 26*(3):429, 1961.

Bortz, Edward L.: Retirement and the Individual. *J Am Geriatr Soc, 16:* 1, 1968.

Bultena, Gordon, and Wood, Vivian: Normative attitudes toward the aged role among migrant and nonmigrant retirees. *Gerontologist, 9:*204, 1969.

Bultena, Gordon L., and Wood, Vivian: The American retirement community: Bane or blessing? *J Gerontol, 24*(2):   , 1969.

Burgess, E. W.: *The Retirement Village.* Ann Arbor, University of Michigan, Division of Gerontology, 1961.

Carp, Frances M. (Ed.): *The Retirement Process.* United States Department of Health, Education, and Welfare, Washington, D.C., 1968.

Carp, Frances M.: housing and minority-group elderly. *Gerontologist, 9:*20, 1969.

Carp, Frances M.: Some components of disengagement. *J Gerontol, 23:*383, 1968.

Carp, Frances M. (Ed.): *Retirement: Frameworks for Research.* San Francisco, Jossey-Bass, 1969.

Carp, Frances M. (Ed.): *The Retirement Process.* Washington, Government Printing Office, 1968.

Charles, Don C.: Effect of participation in a pre-retirement program. *Gerontologist, 22:*24, 1971.

Chen, Yung-Ping: Low income, early retirement, and tax policy, *Gerontologist, 6:*35, 1966.

Christ, Edwin A.: The 'retired' stamp collector: Economic and other functions of systematized leisure activity. In Rose, Arnold, and Peterson, Warren (Eds.): *Older People and Their Social World.* Philadelphia, F. A. Davis, 1965, pp. 93-112.

Christison, J. A.: *Emphasis on Living, A Manual on Retirement Housing.* Valley Forge, Judson Press, 1970.

Clark, M. Margaret: Cultural factors in aging adjustments. Abstract published in *Sanitaria, 12*(6): 11, 1967.

——An anthropological view of retirement. In Carp, Frances (Ed.): *Theoretical Models of the Retirement Process.* publication pending.

Clark, M. Margaret, and Anderson, Barbara G.: *Culture and Aging: An Anthropological Study of Older Americans.* Springfield, Thomas, 1967.

Cottrell, W. Fred, and Atchley, Robert C.: *Women in Retirement: A Preliminary Report.* Oxford, Scripps Foundation, 1968.

Donahue, Wilma, Tibbitts, Clark, Orbach, Harold L., and Pollak, Otto: Retirement: The emerging social pattern. In Tibbitts, Clark (Ed.): *Handbook of Social Gerontology.* Chicago, University of Chicago Press, 1960, pp. 33-406.

Ellison, David L.: Work, retirement and the sick role. *Gerontol, 8:*189, 1968.

Epstein, Lenore A.: Early retirement and work-life experience. *Social Security Bulletin, 29:*3, 1968.

Epstein, Lenore A., and Murray, Janet H.: Employment and retirement. In Neugarten, Bernice L.: *Middle Age and Aging.* Chicago, University of Chicago Press, 1968, pp. 354-356.

Fillenbaum, Gerda H.: On the relation between attitude to work and attitude to retirement. *J Gerontol, 26:*244, 1971.

Friedmann, Eugene, and Havighurst, Robert A.: *The Meaning of Work and Retirement.* Chicago, University of Chicago Press, 1954.

Friedmann, Eugene, and Havighurst, Robert: Can retirement satisfy? In Tibbitts, Clark, (Ed.): *Aging in Modern Society,* pp. 369-375.

Gallaway, Lowell E.: The retirement decision: An exploratory essay. Social Security Administration *Research Report No. 9.* Washington, D.C., U.S. Government Printing Office, 1965.

Gersuny, C.: The rhetoric of the retirement home industry. *Gerontologist, 10:*282, 1970.

Gillespie, Michael: The effect of Residential Segregation on the Social Integration of the Aged. 1967.

Gordon, Margaret s.: Work and Patterns of Retirement. In Kleemeier, Robert W. (Ed.(: *Aging and Leisure*. New York, Oxford University Press, 1961. pp. 15-53.

———Income security programs and the propensity to retirement. In Williams, Richard H., Tibbitts, Clark, and Donahue, Wilma (Eds.): *Processes of Aging*. New York, Atherton Press, 1963, pp. 436-458.

Great Britain Ministry of Pensions and National Insurance: *Reasons for Retiring or Continuing to Work*. London, HMSO, 1954.

Gutmann, David: *Ego Psychological and Developmental Approaches to the 'Retirement Crisis' in Men*. NICHD Retirement Workshop, Washington, D.C., 1967.

Hall, Harold R.: *Some Observations on Executive Retirement*. Cambridge, Harvard University Press, 1954.

Havighurst, Robert J.: Flexibility and the social roles of the retired. *Am J Sociol, 59*(4): , 1954.

Havighurst, Robert J.: Neugarten, Bernice L.; and Bengston, Vern L.: A cross-national study of adjustment to retirement. *Gerontol, 6*:137, 1966.

———*Adjustment to Retirement, A Cross-National Study*. Assen, The Netherlands, VanGorcum, 1969.

Heron, Alastair: Retirement attitudes among industrial workers in the sixth decade of life, *Vita Humana*, #152, 1963.

Heusinkveld, Helen, and Musson, Noverre: *1001 Best Places to Live When You Retire*. Chicago, Dartnell, 1964.

Heyman, Dorothy K., and Jeffers, Frances C.: Wives and retirement: A pilot study. *J Gerontol, 23*:488, 1968.

Hochschild, Arlie Russel: *The Unexpected Community*. Englewood Cliffs, Prentice Hall, 1973.

Hoyt, G. C.: The life of the retired in a trailer park. *Am J Sociol 59*:361, 1954.

Jacobs, Jerry: *Fun City: An Ethnographic Study of a Retirement Community*. New York, Holt, Rinehart, and Winston, 1974.

Jaffe, A. J.: Differential patterns of retirement by social class and personal characteristics. In Carp, Frances M. (Ed.): *The Retirement Process*. United States Department of Health, Education, and Welfare, Washington, D.C., 1968, pp. 105-110.

Johnson, S. K.: *Idle Haven: Community Building Among the Working Class Retired*. Berkeley, University of California Press, 1971.

Korokhoff, Alan: Husband wife expectations and reactions to retirement. In Simpson, Ida, *et al.* (Eds.): *Social Aspects of Aging*. Durham, Duke University Press, 1966.

———*Family patterns and morale in retirement. In Simpson, Ida and McKinney, John C.: Social Aspects of Aging*. Durham, Duke University Press, 1966, pp. 173-192.

King, Charles E., and Howell, William H.: Role characteristics of flexible and inflexible retired persons. *Sociol Soc Res, 49*:153, 1965.

Kleemeier, R. W.: The use and meaning of time in special settings: Retirement communities, homes for the aged, hospitals and other group settings. In Kleemeier, Robert (Ed.): *Aging and Leisure.* New York, Oxford University Press, 1961, pp. 273-308.

____Moosehaven: Congregate living in a community of the retired. *Am J Sociol, 59,*347, 1954.

Kreps, Juanita M.: *Employment, Income, and Retirement Problems of the Aged.* Durham, Duke University, 1963.

____(Ed.) *Technology, Manpower, and Retirement Policy.* Cleveland, World Publishing Co., 1966.

____*Comparative studies of work and retirement. In Shanas, Ethel, and Madge, John (Eds.): Methodology Problems in Cross-National Studies in Aging.* New York, S. Karger, 1968, pp. 75-99.

Lambert, Edouard: Reflections on a policy for retirement. *Int Labor Rev, 90:*365, 1964.

Lipman, Aaron: Role conceptions of couples in retirement. In Tibbitts, Clark *Et al.* (Eds.): *Social and Psychological Aspects of Aging,* New York, Columbia University Press, 1962.

Loether, Herman J.: The meaning of work and adjustment to retirement. In Shostak, Arthur, and Gomberg, William (Eds.): *Blue Collar World: Studies of the American Worker.* Englewood cliffs, Prentice-Hall, 1964, pp. 525-533.

Lowenthal, Marjorie Fiske: Some social dimensions of psychiatric disorders in old age. In Williams, R. H., Tibbitts, C., and Donahue, Wilma (Eds.): *Processes of Aging: Social and Psychological Perspectives.* New York, Atherton Press, 1963, vol II, pp. 224-246. Also published in condensed form in Tibbitts, C., and Donahue, Wilma, (Eds.): *Social and Psychological Aspects of Aging.* New York, Columbia University Press, 1962, pp. 553-554.

____Perspective for Leisure and retirement. In Brockband, Reed, and Wesby-Gibson, Dorothy (Eds.): *Mental Health in a Changing Community.* New York, Grune and Stratton, 1966, pp. 118-126.

____Life Cycle Approach to the Study of Retirement. In Carp, Frances (Ed.): *Conceptual Models of the Retirement Process* (working title). Also Some potentialities of a life cycle approach to the study of retirement. In Carp, Frances (Ed.): *Theoretical Models of the Retirement Process.* San Francisco, Jossey-Bass, Inc., pending.

Lowenthal, Marjorie Fiske, and Boler Deetje: Voluntary vs. involuntary social withdrawal. *J Gerontol, 20:*363, 1965.

Maddox, George L.: Retirement as a social event in the United States. In Neugarten, Bernice L. (Ed.): *Middle Age and Aging.* Chicago, University of Chicago Press, 1968, pp. 357-365.

Martin, John, and Doran, Ann: Evidence Concerning the Relationship Between Health and Retirement. *Sociol Rev, 14:*329-343, 1966.

Mathiasen, Geneva (Ed.): *Criteria for Retirement.* New York, Putman & Sons, 1952.

McEwan, Peter J. M., and Sheldon, Alan P.: Patterns of retirement and related variables. *J Geriatr Psychiatry, 3*:35, 1969.

Monk, Abraham: Factors in the preparation for retirement by middle-aged adults. *Gerontologist, 11*:348, 1971.

Moore, Elon H.: Professors in retirement. In *Research on Aging*. Proceedings of a conference held on August 7-10. UC-Berkeley. Pacific Coast Committee on Old Age Research, Social Science Research Council, 1963.

Myers, Robert J.: Factors in interpreting mortality after retirement. *J Am Statistical Assoc, 49*:499, 1954.

Nadelson, Theodore: A survey of the literature on the adjustment of the aged to retirement. *J Geriatr Psychiatry, 3*:3, 1969.

Orbach, Harold: Normative aspects of retirement. In Tibbitts, Clark, and Donahue, Wilma (Eds.):*Social and Psychological Aspects of Aging*. New York, Columbia University Press, 1962.

Owen, John P., and Belzung, L. D.: Consequences of voluntary early retirement: A case study of a new labour force phenomenon. *Br J Indust Relations, 5*:162, 1967.

Palmore, Erdman B.: Differences in the retirement patterns of men and women. *Gerontologist, 5*:4, 1965.

——Why do people retire? *Aging and Human Development, 2*:269, 1971.

——Retirement patterns among aged men; Findings of the 1963 survey of the aged. *Social Security Bulletin*, xxvii, pp. 3-15.

Peterson, J. A., and Larson, A. E.: Social-psychological factors in selecting retirement housing. In Carp, F. M., and Burnett, W. M.(Eds.): *Patterns of Living and Housing of Middle-Aged and Older People*. Public Health Service Publication No. 1496. Washington, U.S. Government Printing Office, 1966, 129-143.

Pollak, Otto: *The Social Aspects of Retirement*. Pension Research Council, Wharton School of Finance and Commerce, University of Pennsylvania, Illinois, Irwin, Inc., 1956.

Pollman, A. William: Early Retirement: Relationship to variation in life satisfaction. *Gerontologist, 11*:43, 1971.

Early retirement: A comparison of poor health to other retirement factors. *J Gerontol 26*:41, 1971.

Poor Health Not Result, But Cause of Retirement, Missouri Study Finds. *Aging*, 173-174, 11-12, 1969.

Prasad, S. B.: The retirement postulate of the disengagement theory. *Gerontologist, 4*:20, 1964.

Proppe, H.: Housing for the retired and the aged in southern California: An architectural commentary. *Gerontologist, 8*:176, 1968.

Reichard, Suzanne, Livson, Florme, and Petersen, Paul G.: Adjustment to retirement. In Neugarten, Bernice L. (Ed.): *Middle Age and Aged*. Chicago, University of Chicago Press, 1968, pp. 178-180.

Riley, Matilda White, Johnson, Marilyn; and Foner, Anne: *Aging and Society*. vols. I and III,

Rosow, Irving: Retirement housing and social integration. *Gerontologist*, 1(2): Also in Tibbitts, C., and Donahue, W. (Eds.): *Social and Psychological Aspects of Aging*, pp. 325-340.

Sherman, S. R. *et al.:* Psychological Effects of Retirement Housing. *Gerontologist*, 8:170, 1968.

Simpson, Ida H., Back, Kurt W., and McKinney, John C.: Oreintation toward work and retirement, and self-evaluation in retirement. In Simpson, Ida H., and McKinney, John C. (Eds.): *Social Aspects of Aging*. Durham, Duke University Press, 1966, pp. 75-89.

_____Problems of the aging in work and retirement. In Boyd, Rosamonde R., and Oakes, G. C. (Eds.): *Foundations of Practical Gerontology*. Columbia, University of South Carolina Press, 1969, pp. 151-166.

Simpson, Ida H., and McKinney, John C. (Eds.): *Social Aspects of Aging*. Durham, Duke University Press, 1966.

Slavick, Fred, and Wolfbein, Seymour L.: *Compulsory and Flexible Retirement in the American Economy*. Ithaca, Cornell University Press, 1966.

Spence, D. L., and Robinson, Betsy C.: Patterns of retirement in San Francisco. In Carp, Frances (Ed.): *The Retirement Process*. Public Health Service Publication #1779. Washington, D.C., U.S. Government Printing Office, 1968.

Stokes, Randall G., and Maddox, George L.: Some social factors in retirement adaptation. *J Gerontol, 22:*329, 1967.

Streib, Gordon F., and Thompson, Wayne E. (Eds.): Adjustment in retirement. *J Soc Iss, 14*(2): 1958.

_____Situational determinants: health and economic deprivation in retirment. *J Soc Iss, 14:*18, 1958.

_____Personal and social adjustment in retirement. In Donahue, Wilma and Tibbitts, Clark (Eds.): *The New Frontiers of Aging*. Ann Arbor, University of Michigan Press, 1957, pp. 180-197.

Streib, Gordon F., and Schneider, C. J.: *Retirement in American Society.* Ithaca, Cornell University Press, 1971.

_____Family Patterns in Retirement. *J Soc Iss, xiv:*46, 1958.

Thompson, Wayne E.: Pre-retirement anticipation and adjustment in retirement. *J Soc Iss 14:*35, 1958.

Thompson, Wayne E., and Streib, Gordon F., and Kosa, John: The effect of retirement on personal adjustment: A panel analysis. *J Gerontol, 15:*165, 1960.

Tuckman, Jacob, and Lorge, Irving: *Retirement and the Industrial Worker; Prospect and Reality*. New York, Columbia University Teacher's College, 1953.

Tyhurst, James S. *et al.:* Mortality, morbidity and retirement. *Am J Public Health, XLVII,*1437, 1957.

Vivrett, W. K.: Designing a retirement community. In Burgess, E. W. (Ed.): *Housing the Elderly in Retirement Communities.* Ann Arbor, University of Michigan, Division of Gerontology, 1960.

Walkley, R. P. *et al.*, *Retirement Housing in California*. Berkeley, Diablo Press, 1966.

Walkley, R. P. *et al.*: The California Survey of Retirement Housing. *Gerontologist*, 6:28, 1966.

Webber, Irving L.: The organized social life of the retired: Two Florida communities. *Am J Sociol, LIX*:340, 1954.

Webber, I. L., and Osterbind, C. C.: Types of retirement communities. In Burgess, E. W. (Ed.): *Housing the Elderly in Retirement Communities*. Ann Arbor, University of Michigan, Division of Gerontology, 1960.

Wentworth, Edna C.: *Employment After Retirement: A Study of Post-entitlement Work Experience of Men Drawing Benefits Under Social Security*. Washington, D.C., U.S. Government Printing Office, 1968.

Wilner, D. M. *et al.*: Demographic characteristics of residents of planned retirement housing. *Gerontologist, 8*, 164, 1968.

Wolfbein, Seymour L.: *Work Force and Retirement Trends in the Older Population*. Paper prepared for the 8th International Congress of Gerontology, 1969.